THE
CUTTY SARK AND *THERMOPYLAE*
ERA OF SAIL

Cutty Sark and *Thermopylae*, in Sydney Harbour, 1873, painting by Oswald Brett,
F.A.S.M.A., in the possession of Dr. Joan Redshaw, A.M.,
(Courtesy of John Cross, Director of State Archives of New South Wales).

The
Cutty Sark and *Thermopylae*
Era of Sail

By
CYRIL L. HUME and MALCOLM C. ARMSTRONG

GLASGOW
BROWN, SON & FERGUSON, LTD., NAUTICAL PUBLISHERS
4-10 DARNLEY STREET G41 2SD

First Edition – 1987

ISBN 0 85174 500 8

© 1987 BROWN, SON & FERGUSON, LTD., GLASGOW G41 2SD
Made and Printed in Great Britain

CONTENTS

THE

CUTTY SARK and *THERMOPYLAE*

CHINA TEA — AUSTRALIAN WOOL

By Cyril L. Hume
and Malcolm C. Armstrong

TWO famous and celebrated "China Birds" as the tea clippers were affectionately known, grace the waters of Port Jackson. Many visiting sailing ship masters eulogised Sydney harbour as the finest in the world, a paradise as it undoubtedly was, with its unspoiled foreshores, the bottle and glass formation east of Neilsen Park still intact, and with Garden Island in a virginal state with its heavily timbered twin hills.

Cutty Sark and *Thermopylae* first met in Australian waters in March 1873 which event caused excited comment from the Sydney newspapers.

A report reads: "The *Cutty Sark* one of the celebrated tea clippers arrived yesterday from Melbourne after a passage of six days and will take in a cargo of Bulli coal for Shanghai. She is a very fine ship and her performances prove her to be a remarkably fast vessel. Her antagonist *Thermopylae* is in the stream within a few hundred yards of her and no two finer ships for speed have ever visited this port".

PREFACE

THE time is now appropriate for the history of the clipper ship era to be retold. Each succeeding generation appears to have little knowledge of the romantic days of the racing clippers which played a vital part in the development of the Australian colonies.

The activities associated with the 1988 Australian bi-centenary with the redevelopment of Circular Quay and The Rocks area give an indication of an awakening period of the now historic 19th century. This book is intended to be for the enquiring minds of those people who seek to know more and also as a guide line for artists.

FOREWORD

IT is a great pleasure to write a foreword to this excellent history of those colourful and hard-driven, nineteenth-century clippers, engaged in the China tea and Australian wool trade. To those of the younger generation, not conversant with these magnificent, square-rigged vessels, this book should also prove to be an authoritative and fascinating introduction. We should all be reminded that it was through the voyages of such wind-driven ships as these that Australia was first discovered and later settled; this nation is not only in their debt, but is also their memorial.

Cyril Hume, a formidable maritime scholar, is an indefatigable seeker after knowledge and graphic records of these lofty vessels. He was able to obtain priceless information about their build, rig, and other characteristics, from men who had served in them; masters, mates, and seamen, when such men were still living a half century ago. At the same time the author made a first-hand study of the surviving handful of latter-day square-rigged carriers—Finns and Germans—still active in Australian waters between the wars, hauling grain to Europe. This book with its unique collection of rare photographs splendidly enhancing the text, is a valuable contribution to maritime history.

The author has also constructed models of the CUTTY SARK and THERMOPYLAE, two of the finest and swiftest sailing vessels ever built. The models themselves are also considered to be amongst the world's finest. The model of the THERMOPYLAE is unique. It incorporates data derived from old sailors who had formerly sailed in this famous vessel, both before and abaft the mast. There was no known deck plan extant of the THERMOPYLAE, and it was only possible to painstakingly reconstruct all these missing deck details and features from this original source. These deck details, before being irretrievably lost, are now enshrined in two flawlessly fashioned models. Both models are in public collections; one in Sydney and the other in Melbourne.

It has been my good fortune to have known Cyril Hume and his work for upwards of forty-five years. I have been privileged to watch him at work, meticulously crafting with infinite patience and utter fidelity, the numerous fittings, masts, spars and rigging details which contribute to the completion of a model. Cyril Hume is an inspired and dedicated artist, and the same untiring effort which goes into his models has also been devoted to the writing of this absorbing and eminently readable account of the brave clipper era. May it encounter fair winds, and a truly prosperous voyage.

Oswald L. Brett, F.A.S.M.A.
LONG ISLAND, NEW YORK
April 25, 1981.

ACKNOWLEDGEMENTS

IT gave me great pleasure to assist Cyril Hume with this book, but it is very sad that he did not live to see it published. Cyril Hume wrote the basic manuscript in 1979, but it was four years later when I became involved and together we took positive steps to complete the work with a selection of photographs from Cyril's personal archives, The manuscript had only been in the hands of the publishers for a few weeks when Cyril died. As the culmination to a lifetime study of sailing ships and seamen, Cyril was very excited at the prospect of seeing this book in print. His collection of memorabilia is now at the Sydney Maritime Museum, but I am sure he would be pleased to know that his book is now available to give pleasure to people all over the world.

Cyril Hume expressed his grateful thanks to his friend Doreen M. Walsh for her dedicated assistance in preparing the original manuscript.

The photographs of *"Thermopylae"* sailing as a barque under the Canadian flag (page 42) and in dry dock at Esquimalt on Vancouver Island (page 40) are from the Provincial Archives of British Columbia (catalogue Nos 10716 and 39460 respectively).

The two photographs of the ship *"Samuel Plimsoll"* and one of *"Samuel Plimsoll"*'s figurehead (pages 77, 79, 80) came from the State Library of South Australia .

Our thanks go to Mr. Karl Kortum and the San Francisco Maritime Museum for the photographs of the four masted barque *"Bermuda"* (page 160), the *Antiope* shown with sail damage in San Francisco (page 140) and the group of masters and mates in the San Francisco Navigation School (page 158).

All of the photographs in the book are from Cyril Hume's personal collection, that he had acquired from many sources over many years. The origin of most of them is obscure and was impossible to determine after his death. If there are other sources who feel they were due an acknowledgement for any photographs included in the book I can only hope that they will realise they have not been left out deliberately.

The Discharge Certificate of R. B. McKilliam is reproduced courtesy of his son, Mr. R. L. McKilliam of Sydney (page 74).

The tea stowage illustration (page 4) appears in "Stevens on Stowage" 6th edition published in 1873.

The six paintings by Jack Spurling were first published by the Blue Peter Publishing Company of London and have been photographed from the books SAIL, volumes I and II, published in 1927 and 1929 respectively.

Our thanks also go to marine artists Oswald Brett and David Hogan for the reproduction of their paintings. My own paintings in this book were done specifically for inclusion at Cyril Hume's request and he saw most of them completed before he died. *Cutty Sark, Thermopylae, Halloween* and *Marco Polo* were among his favourite ships.

Both Cyril and I want to thank my wife Marie who has put in many hours of patient assistance with research, art work, checking and reading; in particular, Cyril wanted her to be thanked for her work on the flags.

I would have preferred to have been simply mentioned here by Cyril Hume for having assisted with his book, I wish he could see it completed and I had not expected to be playing such a big part in its production. On behalf of everyone interested in ships, the sea and maritime history I think it is fitting that I should acknowledge Cyril Hume's contribution to our knowledge and enjoyment.

MALCOLM C. ARMSTRONG, F.AUS.I.N., F.N.I.

THE CHINA TEA TRADE

THE history of the tea-trade goes back to the 17th century when tea was brought into Europe by the Dutch India ships and small quantities were transhipped to London. Tea had been brought to Portugal from Macao, their port on the China coast and was familiar to Catherine of Braganza, wife of Charles II, so was introduced to the English Court. At over 100 shillings per pound, it was available only to the very wealthy. Such was the beginning of tea drinking in England, under most auspicious circumstances which ultimately led to the traditional "cup o' tea".

During the latter half of the 17th century, the London East Company began to import tea, but, having a monopoly on the trade, their imports of tea were slow and frustrating. However, by 1840 China ports were open for free trade. By this time Americans were developing fast sailing ships, and their new Clipper *Oriental* was making fast passages from Ohira to New York. This so impressed the English merchants that they chartered her to take tea to London. *Oriental* made a fast passage of 97 days. This so excited the London merchants that the English and Scottish ship designers and builders decided to meet the challenge. From their yards began an era of clipper ships of speed and with beauty of form that lasted until 1869 when the Suez Canal was opened. Tea steamers then entered the trade and were able to halve the time from the China ports to London. The lengthy passage around the Cape of Good Hope was eliminated. Speed was essential as the merchants who received the first cargo of the season's new tea rewarded the owner and master of the clipper with a handsome premium.

1

To have viewed the tea fleet awaiting in ballast for the tea to come down the river, would have been a sheer delight. With their upper strakes of metal sheathing glinting in the sunlight, their topsides glossed without a plank showing, gold sheer strakes reaching from highly ornamented headwork surmounted by pure white figureheads as well as the stern decorations must have been a pleasing sight. Inboard bright work (varnished timber), a profusion of polished brass, and the panelled bulwarks displayed ornate and delicate designs. Aloft there was an impressive overlarge spar plan reaching to the sky with either varnished black or white yards and masts. If anchored in company with her sisters of the tea fleet at the Pagoda Anchorage there was provided a background of splendour and delight.

Chinese stevedores were regarded as the best in the world. Consequently their requirements for the stowage of tea were most meticulous. The holds were thoroughly cleaned, especially if they had carried a coal cargo from an Australian port. The permanent ballast was usually granite. Sydney sandstone had been tried but was found to hold too much moisture. On top of the tiers of granite, river-bed shingle was laid by hand, in tiers, with the exact height required to the deck beams above, determined by measuring rods to allow the stowage of the correct number of tea boxes each tier being measured in the same way. Small spaces were occupied by small boxes, 14"×12". If a box protruded slightly, a Chinaman with a large well-cushioned posterior, was required to stand off and take a running jump on to the top of the box. This was effective apparently. (Did he receive the "bottom" rate of pay?)

At Foochow, stocks from the tea gardens would accumulate until the Chinese merchants were prepared to sell at a price acceptable to the great Hongs or Merchant houses (such as Jardine Matheson & Co.). After much haggling, a price was agreed upon and the deal closed whereupon the other Hongs or Houses would also commence buying. Speed was then the order of the day, to have the boxes weighed and labelled and loaded into lighters to be taken down river to the waiting clippers at the Pagoda anchorage 10 miles away, awaiting to receive their

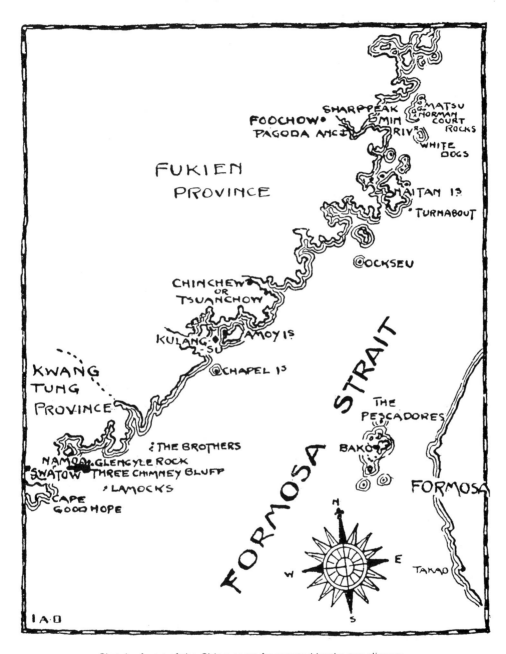

Sketch of part of the China coast frequented by the tea clippers.

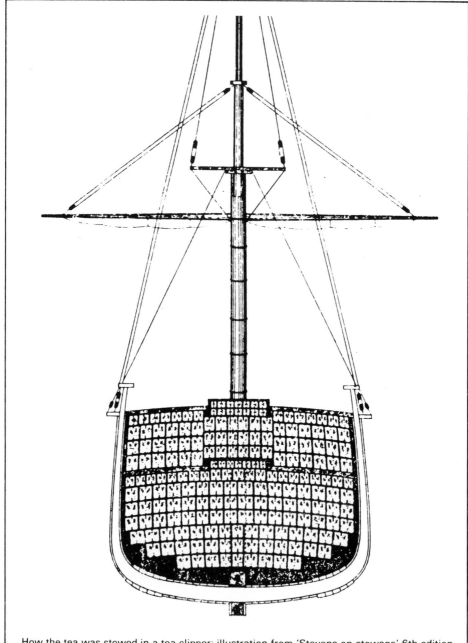

How the tea was stowed in a tea clipper; illustration from 'Stevens on stowage' 6th edition published in 1873.

"chops". (A "chop" was a number of boxes of the same variety and quality of tea and, generally, the product of one particular garden. The word "chop" is also used in the term "Chop-boat", that is, a vessel with a capacity of 500 chests, used to take the tea to the waiting clipper).

With the crews on the clippers standing by, the sails bent to the yards, gear rove off, the agents' flags flying aloft, a distant sound would be heard up river. As the hullabaloo increased, the whole scene became colourful activity as the Lorches and lighters were warped alongside the clippers, with double gangs of coolies on board waiting to stow the fragrant tea below. After completion of loading, with the Blue Peter flying aloft, the clippers lost no time in being in readiness for the perilous passage down the Min river with its narrow gorge, submerged rocks and treacherous currents. The pilots were dropped at the island of Matsu.

Once at sea, there were further hazards caused by the deadly menace of piracy. The well-found clippers were always well armed and ready for any attack. The fact that they were so, was an effective deterrent (spies on the China coast would have been well aware of that). Nevertheless, there were losses, such as the *Caliph* built at Aberdeen in 1870. She went missing without a trace of any kind. Although she was believed to have been the fastest of them all, it was assumed that she was lost to pirates.

The tea-clipper *Childers* came to grief on a shore and fell victim to a large group of fishermen who seized the opportunity to gather around the clipper. After inviting the crew to depart from the scene without delay the fishermen stripped the clipper of everything that was moveable; they took even the top strakes of the metal bottoming of the hull.

Sometimes, a ship's chronometer or bell would be found in a junk shop on Endicott Lane in Hong Kong. If the culprits were traced and caught, punishment was swift. They were hanged from a handy tree.

If a rich pirate was caught, he was allowed to buy a "stand-in" who by being willing to make such a sacrifice, showed tremendous devotion to his family. His life was exchanged for a large sum of money for the benefit of his aged parents. Filial devotion at

The *Black Prince*, shortly after her launching at Aberdeen. She was a typical China tea clipper, but never allowed to show her paces because of a very cautious master.

The yacht like hull of the tea clipper *Osaka* accentuates the form of a china bird.

The *Wild Deer,* a splendid clipper engaged in China tea trade and later in the wool trade. Photographed here at Port Chalmers in New Zealand.

The forecastle crowd of the *Wild Deer, enjoying* having their photograph taken.

its best! Pirates were meted out quick execution by the port authorities. They were lined up on a nearby beach, trussed like fowls, their hands behind their backs lashed to their ankles. The executioner with an assistant, moved along the line, and, with a sweep of his sword, lopped off each head in turn. There was always a gallery of onlookers who would no doubt absorb an effective deterrent.

In 1878, the authorities at Swatow were concerned about the activities of pirates in the area. They were eventually tracked down to a quaintly named spot—"The Three Chimney Bluff". Three shafts were discovered, leading below to a large cave, where twenty pirates were captured. The cave was found to be full of loot such as compasses, binnacles, ships' bells and many other ship fittings. The pirates were executed, except for the pirate chief and his sons who were bricked up alive in the "Three Chimneys", there to ponder on their dark deeds of the past.

Once at sea the clippers lost no time in setting all possible sail for the London Markets 13,000 miles away. Seas and weather allowing, studding sails were sent aloft. Additional sails were set such as a Jamie Green under the head sails; a ring tail on the spanker, lower stunsails on the fore with topsail and topgallants on both sides fore and main. Sometimes a water sail was set under the fore lower studding sail. A veritable cloud of canvas for fine weather sailing but not for raging seas.

As the racing tea clippers had reached the pinnacle of perfection in ship design, so did their masters in seamanship. To handle a tea clipper required courage, endurance and nerves of steel. No clipper would have reached fame without these qualities in her master. Once at sea, the master, was the man to drive the ship,

The ship *Halloween*, as did *Cutty Sark*, added great prestige to the clipper fleet of John Willis and proved to be a most successful iron clipper when she created a record from Shanghai to London in 89 days in 1873. The photograph shows her at the foot of Pitt Street, Sydney, in 1871 with a rig similar to that of *Cutty Sark* and flying an enormous house flag.

Waiting for tea cargo at the Pagoda anchorage in China; the ship in the foreground is probably *Ariel*.

handle the officers and crew and dedicate himself to the mighty task ahead. The racing crews were handpicked, all A.B.s who took great pride in their respective ships. Year by year the passage from China became a closely contested race, through the China Seas, down the Indian Ocean, around the Cape of Good Hope and then up the long leg of the Atlantic, often not knowing how the other ships were faring. In the famous 1866 race, the two leaders *Ariel* and *Taeping*, did not sight each other until they reached the English Channel. *Ariel* was declared the winner although *Taeping* with a stronger tug docked 20 minutes before *Ariel*. Captain Watchlin who was the third mate of *Taeping*, was adamant that his ship had won the race. However the race was declared a dead heat and prize money was divided. A fair decision! Captain Watchlin's share of the prize money was £100.

Some of the best known of the China tea clippers were *Ariel, Taeping, Sir Lancelot* (the record holder), *Spindrift, Taitsing, Norman Court, Titania, Serica, Fiery Cross, Lothair, Kaisow* and *Halloween* (record holder from Shanghai to London). In 1868 *Thermopylae* joined the fleet to be followed a year later by *Cutty Sark*.

Tea clipper, *Kaisow*

The ship *Lahloo*, shows her lovely hull form; a beautiful bow, graceful and artistic sheer line to the bird-tail stern. The twin funnels belong to a tug alongside.

WOOL TRADE

THE dramatic expansion of the early Australian wool industry commenced at about the time that free immigration superceded the predominance of the convict era. As the settlers moved inwards from the coastal areas over plain and mountain into new country with their flocks of sheep, so did the Australian wool begin to dominate the European markets.

Dalgety's wool store at Darling Harbour, Sydney. A wool wagon has arrived as the bales are being hoisted into the store bales ready for shipment, are coming down a chute to the barrowman to be loaded onto the ship.

A forest of masts and spars at Millers Point in Sydney, in 1882. The ship in the foreground is the Loch Tyne with her main yard and crojack yard cockbilled for loading wool; next to her is the ship *Trafalgar*.

The figurehead of *Loch Tay,* looking over a smoky Port Adelaide, appears to be contemplating the glories of sail.

The ship *Derwent,* under sail.

Derwent, at anchor with yards squared, awaiting her cargo.

This photograph of the *Sara Grice*, shows the type of stunsails boom in vogue during the 1870's.

In England, the declining wool industry could not cope with the demand from the wool staplers of Leeds and Manchester. Attention was turned towards the new silky wool that was coming from Saxony where growers had been crossing their sheep with Spanish Merinos since the beginning of the 19th century and producing wool extremely soft and fine. This completely out-classed the English wool, bringing the English industry close to ruin. Prior to this, Australian wool that had reached England was regarded as a curiosity of no importance and even a source of amusement, referred to as "Botany Bay wool". But from the time that John Macarthur's lone bale of wool reached England in 1807, it became evident over the years that the quality was steadily improving. Other growers, as well as Macarthur, were producing a wool that was quite as silky and as good for combing as the best Electoral flocks of Saxony.

There was a time when rivalry in sheep-breeding between U.K. and the Continent was so important that the smuggling of lambs across the Channel became a hanging matter in England. Hence the expression, "as well be hanged for a sheep as a lamb".

The road to Bennelong Point and Fort Macquarie, (now the site of Sydney Opera House). The brig is shown handling wool in the coastal trade and an Aberdeen clipper, possibly *Ninevah*, is about to receive her wool cargo for the long passage to London.

A crowded shipping scene at Port Adelaide; the *Northern Belle* is in the foreground.

Superior felting and combing qualities were demanded and Australian wool came on the scene to offer these. It was longer, softer and silkier than any except the very best Saxon and was ideal for the upper-grade cloths required. London merchants predicted a complete triumph for the soft wool of Australia and the ultimate results more than justified their opinion.

In 1822, Australia sent only 175,000 pounds of wool to England. By 1839, Australian exports were up to 10 million pounds of wool a year. Australia was then the second largest exporter of wool to England, second only to Germany. This meant a struggle for supremacy between the two countries, the objective being to cover the whole range in quality and quantity.

The odds were against Australia especially when the protective Navigation Laws were repealed thus exposing the colonies to the competition of free trade. The scientific Saxon farmers were confident that they could more than hold their own but they went too far in their breeding techniques. Their sheep certainly had an extremely fine fleece but were almost useless otherwise. The sheep was a physical weakling, deficient in meat, vigour and quality of wool. Realising that their sheep should be a variety that covered the whole range, they produced a "reconstructed" Merino that appeared to be a serious challenge to the Australian sheep. But it was impossible to compete with the expanding background of the Australian environment. The sheep in Australia did not require tending and nursing but had the wide warm plains on which to spread. They did not need protective attention in the

A familiar trader to Australian waters *Star of Peace*, built in 1885; seen here at Circular Quay East about the mid 60's. A unique feature of the ship is the Cunningham's patent reefing topsails. The yards could be revolved from the deck, rolling up the sails like window blinds.

c

Miltiades, a well known wool carrier of the Aberdeen line.

Torridon, a very well known wool carrier displays action with sails filled; wind on starboard quarter with yards corkscrewed to gain a little more power from the wind.

warm climate of this vast land. Sheepmen were already beyond the Murray and the Monaro areas; they had extended past New England converging on to the Darling Downs and the flockmasters of the south were rolling on around the Murrumbidgee. Tasmania was developing a wool industry as was South Australia. This southern continent had the land and the climate. Germany could not compete. By 1850 Australia was producing over 130,000 bales annually to Germany's 30,000 bales. The New World had defeated the Old to the extent that by 1845 the buyers in Germany were importing wool from Australia in large quantities.

Australia was faced with the problem of shipping the wool to the London markets in the fastest time possible in order to beat what has been aptly called "The Tyranny of Distance". Providentially, the 1840's saw the advent of what was to become known as the era of the Clipper ship. The meaning of the word "Clipper" has not been clearly defined. The American Historian, Carl C. Cutler, declares that the term was in use by 1835 in books of travel and in works of fiction. David Macgregor of England has noted the use of the word in 1819, but, generally speaking, the Clipper era belongs to the time between the 1840's and the 1880's. The clippers were built with the attributes of a hull with a short entrance, a fine run aft and were heavily sparred with a large sail area for the purpose of speed.

Loch Vennachar, one of the famous Loch Line Ships.

A sailing ship master's nightmare: allmost a flat calm with the captain on deck whistling for a wind. The ship is the wool carrier *Argonaut.*

Captain Holmes, master of the *Cimba,* a well known and celebrated seaman.

Ship *Cimba,* well known in the wool trade.

The enterprising and skilful photographers of the 60's and later years produced magnificent images of the Clippers berthed around Circular Quay, Sydney, each with its own loading ramp on which to roll the bales of wool towards the holds. The spectacular horse-drawn wool wagons were seen in increasing numbers at the wharves and all classes of ships were carrying a quota of wool. River-craft and coastal vessels and also rail transport were all contributing to the pressing demand of transporting the wool to the clippers loading for the London sales. The Quay presented a moving scene with a dozen or more clipper ships berthed alongside awaiting their cargoes. To the seafarer, there was no more exciting port of call than Sydney Harbour. Passenger and

The *Great Victoria*, ex *General Jacquard*, is another photograph that has been published many times, but not the details. The photographer is believed to be Allerding, who always employed a hansom cab (in foreground), to carry his gear for the laborious wet plate process. Built at Nantes, as a steam powered auxiliary, the vessel transported troops to the Crimean war, from France. Stunsail booms are aloft on the foremast. The North Shore ferry *Waratah*, is in the foreground and the tower of Saint Phillips dominates the Sydney skyline.

A rare photograph of the West side of the Rocks area, Sydney; the original was at least three feet square, the above is a segment. (Negative was accidently torn in the 1930's). The ships are believed to be *William Duthie* and *Seraphis*.
(Acknowledgement to N.S.W. Government printer for this photograph).

Work horses of the Australian coastal trade, with *Jessie Kelly*,
in the foreground. Darling Harbour, Sydney, 1871.

immigrant ships were also berthed in this great harbour. It must
have been a joy to behold.

The wool clippers, berthed close to the agents' warehouses,
were loaded as quickly as possible. There was tremendous activity
with the stevedores sweating to screw as many bales into the hold
as could be, right up to the deck beams. With the hatches battened
down, the crews would be seen sitting astride the yards, bending
the sails in preparation for their departure through Sydney Heads
on the long, arduous and hazardous voyage around Cape Horn, to
the London Sales.

Campbell's Wharf, Sydney, judging by the rig of the ships possibly in the 1850's. The ships represent the class whose voyages lasted about 120 days. The single topsail yards, proclaim their early vintage as double topsails came into use in the 1860's.

"You can dunnage casks o' tallow; you can
    handle hides an' horn;
You can carry frozen mutton; you can lumber
    sacks o' corn;
But the queerest kind o' cargo that you've got to
    haul and pull
Is Australia's 'staple product'—is her God—
    abandoned wool.
For it's greasy an' its stinkin', an' them awkward
    ugly bales.
Must be jammed as close as herrings in a ship afore
    she sails".

From the poem "Laying on the Screw" by E. J. Brady.

Interesting as Circular Quay is today, the occasional visit by a sailing ship adds the romance and glamour that is reminiscent of the past era of the wool fleet. During the middle decades of the nineteenth century, before the ferry wharves were built, as many as fourteen or fifteen ships would have been berthed alongside. There was an atmosphere that was exciting and intimate; with an intermingling of Masters and sailors alike, with the Sunday crowds that blocked the Quay, to inspect the ships, to talk to the officers and crews, to hear the latest news from England and to listen to fo'c'sle-head "sing-songs" from the latest music-hall ditties.

During 1868 the clipper *Ben Lomond* was tied alongside the Quay and her young Master married the daughter of the superintendent of the A.S.N. Co. To celebrate the occasion, every vessel around the Quay 'dressed up' with a tremendous profusion

Aviemore, tied up to the bank at the S. E. corner of Circular Quay in 1871. In spite of the wet plates process with long exposure, the camera lenses were of excellent quality and a lot of detail can be seen in this photograph. *Aviemore,* was the last wooden ship built by Hood for the Aberdeen Line. An apprentice is aloft, on the mizzen lower top sail yard enjoying the view. Stock pens are ashore and the loading ramp is ready for receiving cargo.

Clipper ship *Brilliant*.

Captain and officers of *Brilliant*.

Brilliant, making port minus topgallant and royal masts on main and mizzen.

of flags and bunting flying. What more fitting tribute could a seafaring bridegroom and his bride receive?

Many famous travellers were lost in admiration at the Sydney Harbour scene. One, the celebrated nautical writer and seaman, Joseph Conrad, gave this word picture: "The night has closed down rapidly. Sitting here on the rail of the bow at Circular Quay I look over one of the finest, most beautiful, vast and safe bays the sun ever shone upon. I look up the short street and I can hear the seamen of the fleet celebrating in the 'King's Head': and the voice

Torrens, at Port Adelaide after striking an iceberg.

of the many crying 'Hot saveloys' at the end of George Street where the cheap eating houses are kept by Chinamen—tomorrow will be Sunday and to these ships whose names have attained the dignity of household words, will come the citizens bent on visiting. And, it will fall on me, Joseph Conrad, the officer on duty, to play guide, especially to the citizenesses—and out of the stern ports will float the tinkle of more or less untuned cottage pianos, till the gas lamps begin to twinkle on the streets and the ship's nightwatchmen haul down the flags and fasten a brighter lamp at the break of the gangway''

Before the wool started coming down from the country areas the ships began to gather and it was no unusual sight to see some twenty full-rigged ships anchored below Garden Island. There was keen rivalry to be regarded as the smartest ship. As a result, every yard was trimmed to a hair's breadth, hulls and spars were freshly painted, decks were holystoned until they were as white as snow and every piece of brasswork was polished until it dazzled the eyes. Captain Phillips, when mate of the clipper *Brilliant* , would stand ahead in a boat and direct the squaring of the yards by means of a flag in each hand. The harbour shore residents were captivated by the dogwatch chanties of the waiting crews of the clippers soon to be racing away. One crew would start up, and, ship by ship, others would follow suit to the vast enjoyment of the listeners on shore. Little wonder that visiting seamen from all parts of the globe regarded Sydney Harbour as a Veritable Paradise on earth.

Circular Quay has acquired, in spite of the changing scene, an air of romance that has lived on from one generation to another.

Blackadder, was built off the plans as a sister ship, to *Halloween*, for the fleet of John Willis, in the China tea trade. For the first few years, the clipper was most unlucky from broken gear and dismasting. After surviving many mishaps, she made some fine passages. In this scene at Millers Point, Sydney, her main yard is cockbilled for hoisting cargo from a lighter alongside.

THERMOPYLAE,

THE PRIDE OF THE BRITISH MERCHANT MARINE

IN August 1868, a clipper ship was launched at Aberdeen, Scotland, she was to gain tremendous prestige for herself and immortality in the romantic story of the great days of sail; her name was *Thermopylae*.

In November the same year she dropped her pilot at Gravesend in the English Channel and 60 days later signalled for a pilot off Port Phillip Heads, Victoria, Australia, a record which still stands to her credit. On the next voyage to Melbourne, she came within a few hours of repeating her maiden run.

These, along with later performances of averaging 67 days for 10 passages from London to Melbourne earned her pride of place in the colourful history of the sailing ships of the British merchant marine, and eventually she became a legend.

Her appearance was flawless and represented the pinnacle of clipper ship design and perfection. *Thermopylae* was noted for a graceful yacht-like hull with green topsides above the yellow metalling of the underwater body, the two top strakes of which were burnished when at anchor in port. She had a rising gold decorated bow surmounted by a pure white figurehead and the pleasing line of the sheer accentuated by a gold strake, level with the main deck and a brass edged t'gallant rail above tapering aft to a shapely bird tail stern.

Above, a tremendous tracery of rigging was suspended against the sky by slender white and varnished wooden tapering spars. On deck, a profusion of varnished teak and polished brass work shone in the sunlight, the whole presenting a sight that was a veritable picture of romance and glamour.

This photograph of the *Thermopylae,* is undoubtedly the best likeness of the famous clipper. The original was taken by the photographer Hall of Hunter Street, Sydney, unfortunately the original negative along with a dray full of other negatives was dumped in the harbour about 1900. The original print of which this one is a good copy was in the possession of Captain McKilliam, who was Second Mate at the time, 1882.

Sydney Habour in the 70's. Warships on the Sydney station can be seen in Farm Cove, and *Thermopylae,* is anchored in the stream between Fort MacQuarie and Fort Denison.

The hull form of *Thermopylae* was in keeping with her sisters of the China tea fleet, with a sharply sloping cutwater, a fine entrance and a beautiful run aft, with the emphasis on speed and more speed. This was a requirement to meet the needs of the London merchants to receive the new season's teas from China in the quickest time possible with a premium to be won by the first clipper to dock.

Thermopylae was not expressly designed for the China tea trade but more as a trader for Melbourne to take in a cargo, such as coal for China and then to compete for the new season's teas. It was in these ports such as Foo Chow, when assembled as a fleet, that these beautiful clippers looked their best, with their ensigns and enormous house flags fluttering from the main trucks, topsides and brasswork gleaming in the sun.

The hull of *Thermopylae* was of composite construction as were many of the clippers with wood planking on iron frames and this was the period of transition from all wood to all iron ships. It was a most successful combination as shown by the longevity of such ships as *Sobraon* (1866-1941) broken up in Berry's Bay, Sydney, and *Cutty Sark* preserved for future generations at Greenwich, London, both so well known in the Australian trade. *Thermopylae's* planking was of rock elm from keel to topside, East India teak above, wood deck of four inch thick yellow pine and poop house decking of New Zealand Kauri. The figurehead was of the young King Leonidas, who with shield on left arm and sword arm extended, represented the epic defence to the death against the Persian hordes, of the Pass at Thermopylae 480 B.C. by the small band of Spartans; a magnificent example of the ship carver's art.

The figurehead carver was an artist craftsman whose sculpture from a solid block of wood was a sight much loved by anyone with an eye for a ship, and especially by the seamen.

Unlike the Naval coloured figureheads, most clipper ship owners traditionally painted their figureheads white all over; possibly with the idea that from a distance, the profile of the figure would show up to advantage against the background of sea and sky whereas a coloured one would merge and be lost to view. No one took greater pride in the appearance of their clippers than the owners themselves.

Thermopylae was fortunate in having Captain Kemball for her Master, a seaman with a reputation for driving, full of energy and enterprise, with the daring and courage necesary to handle a racing clipper.

With the mainmast soaring to 145 feet from deck to truck, a mainyard of 80 feet, as compared to length of hull of 212 feet and beam of 35 feet, it is obvious that seamanship had to be at its best, especially with a stun's'l set on either side which extended the sail breadth on the foreyard to 120 feet overall, and with this magnificent spread of canvas she looked like a summer cloud drifting across the ocean.

The clipper carried a picked racing crew of 34 who were kept busy replacing gear and broken stun's'l booms. On the maiden voyage a seaman was washed off the jibboom, in the English Channel and although the ship hove to for an hour, he was not found.

Thermopylae, during the 80's sporting double gallant yards. Sails are furled and after discharging her cargo she will be loaded with bales of wool for the London market.

A painting of *Thermopylae,* by Percival.

Thermopylae, at anchor in Sydney Harbour.

Thermopylae made at least 9 runs of over 350 sea miles a day. She was without peer to windward and probably the only contemporary ship capable of rivalling her speed in strong favouring winds was the *Cutty Sark*.

When *Thermopylae* berthed at Melbourne on completion of her maiden voyage, great interest and admiration for the new clipper was shown by the people of Melbourne. The apprentices were lionised and one convinced a journalist that the ship was such a marvellous sea boat that a grindstone had stood on the deck for the duration of the passage without being lashed down! The claim was partly justified as she proved herself, when in a severe gale in the Bay of Biscay, on a later voyage; the Captain ordered the crew to stand by with axes ready to cut the rigging lanyards to allow the masts to go over the sides, but to the admiration of the crew she came through without this drastic action and righted herself.

Some years ago, an eyewitness to the launching, in a letter to a Melbourne newspaper described how the shipyard hands lined up on deck when she was afloat and in a body ran from side to side to test her stability, with gratifying results for the master shipwright, no doubt.

Once *Thermopylae* demonstrated her weatherly qualities when leaving Melbourne for Newcastle. Her tug cast off two miles below the Gellibrand Lightship. Sail was set and she stood over towards the St. Kilda bank, stayed and on the port tack headed for Point Cook, went around again and fetched the head of the South Channel to the amazement of the pilot, who said that the weatherly qualities of the clipper eclipsed anything that he had seen and added that no square-rigged ship had **ever** made the Channel in three tacks with the wind from the same quarter.

At Newcastle, the clipper loaded coal for Shanghai and created another record of 28 days pilot to pilot, and then joined the tea clipper fleet at Foo Chow lying at the Pagoda anchorage waiting for the new season's teas.

The coast line south of Hong Kong presented a menace to the clippers in the way of piratical attacks from the junks with their murderous crews, who under the cover of darkness would attack any vessel becalmed and unless an effective anchor watch was kept, the crew would be murdered and the ship plundered, fired and sunk.*Thermopylae* was well prepared to repel boarders and carried an effective armoury. It was the duty of apprentice Charles Fyfe, later of North Fitzroy, to clean and oil the weapons. There were two small brass guns lashed to the main deck just for'ard of the break of the poop. Around the mizenmast below deck there was a rack of 20 Tower Hill muskets, 20 cutlasses besides 20 boarding pikes, 20 round shot and 20 grape shot and at least these gave some feeling of security for the crew. Fortunately for all concerned the occasion did not arise for their usage, excepting that the cannons were put to use as signal guns off various ports including Port Phillip.

These were exciting days for the Sunday crowds at Melbourne wharves with the finest sailing ships ever built, as visitors to excite their imagination, and to inspect. Some of *Thermopylae*'s features

Thermopylae, at Vancouver in 1890, awaiting refitting for her Canadian owners.

Thermopylae, in a floating dock at Esquimalt, Vancouver Island, British Columbia, about 1895. Clearly showing her fine run aft. Photograph from archives of Victoria, B.C.

aroused great interest; for instance she carried patent reefing gear on her main t'gallant in the form of a rolling spar mounted on the fore side of the yard. The spar could be revolved from the deck and the sail wound up around it like a roller blind, a very handy contrivance when caught in a squall because instead of sending men aloft, the sail could be furled in a matter of seconds and lessen the possibility of the t'gallant mast going over the side.

During the '80s economies were introduced by the sailing ship owners, owing to the competition of the steamship lines and in 1890 *Thermopylae* was sold to Canadian ownership for £5,000 and continued to maintain her reputation although cut down to barque rig.

Australian ports saw her no more as the trade then, was between Victoria, British Columbia, and the Eastern ports from Tokyo to Singapore. For the first time she had a skipper unworthy of her prestige. This character sold a lifeboat, stun's'l gear and the Tower Hill muskets from the armoury. He was very soon replaced at Singapore by another skipper who, with the mate, lived most of the time in a state of inebriation.

On the voyage to Vancouver the clipper ran into typhoon weather, lost most of her bulwarks. Mains'l, tops'ls and other canvas was blown to pieces, but her cargo of rice was landed in

Thermopylae, at New Westminster, British Columbia.

Thermopylae, sailing as a barque under the Canadian flag she still retained her reputation as a fast sailer.

Thermopylae, as a barque when sold to the Portugese.

good condition. The skipper and his mate, in spite of good seamanship during the typhoon, received the sack when they reached Victoria.

In 1892 *Thermopylae* came into her own again under the command of Captain Winchester, with a fine crew recruited from the *Black Diamond* of British Columbia. Captain Winchester was a superb seaman and soon had the ship showing her paces with some remarkable passages on record. *Thermopylae* was cut down to barque rig and her green hull was painted white.

In 1895 *Thermopylae* was sold to the Portuguese Government who converted her to a training ship and renamed her *Pedro Nunes*.

When her useful career as a training ship came to an end she was towed to sea and torpedoed by units of the Portuguese Navy, watched by the Queen of Portugal. *Thermopylae* dipped her bows to waves for the last time. Her distinguished life was of 39 years and there are many who believe that she was the finest clipper ship ever built.

The sinking of *Thermopylae,* in 1906.

CUTTY SARK,

THE LAST OF THE RACING CLIPPERS

PROMINENT amongst the mid-Victorian ship owners was Captain Jock Willis of London. His father, Captain John Willis, was a ship owner before him and Captain Jock had inherited his fleet of sailing ships. Jock Willis, or "Old White Hat" (a tribute to the immaculate white top hat which he invariably wore) was the last of his kind, sole owner and with a close personal interest in his ships and crews. It was his custom to farewell his ships personally and the apprentices would line the rails, and with raised caps, give their employer a hearty "good-bye

Captain "Gentleman" White and apprentices and others of *The Tweed*.

44

Superb model of *Cutty Sark,* by Sir Maurice Denny of Dumbarton. Near destruction in the bombing of Glasgow, beautifully restored by Lieutenant Commander Waite, of the Greenwich Museum. Believed by the author to be the finest model of the *Cutty Sark* in existance. Original rig as *Cutty Sark* appeared in China trade.

Sir". Old Jock always responded with a cheerful "good-bye my lads".

Thermopylae's record breaking maiden voyage passage to Melbourne determined Captain Jock Willis to have a ship designed to beat her and all other clippers. One of Willis' famous clippers was *The Tweed*, a magnificent ship well-known in the Australian trade. Willis engaged the small firm of Scott and Linton of Dumbarton, to design, and construct his new tea clipper that would beat all others. In 1868 Willis took Linton to see *The Tweed* in dry dock. Possibly, Captain Stuart and Captain Moodie, (previously mate on *The Tweed*) were also present. Their testimony regarding her qualities, Linton's own shrewd judgement, and Willis' feeling for his speedy favourite, resulted in the lines of the bow being incorporated in the design of the new clipper. The agreed price was £16,150, or about £17 per ton.

The story of the *Cutty Sark,* has been rewritten many times and will no doubt be repeated for the benefit of each succeeding generation, as will also this fine photograph. Taken from an elevated position in Potts Point Sydney, it clearly displays the beautiful hull form of the thoroughbred tea clipper with an immense spar plan surmounted by the *Cutty Sark* emblem at her main truck which also served as a wind vane. How splendid indeed that such a likeness of *Cutty Sark,* has survived for posterity.

Hercules Linton produced an inspired design which included a powerful stern that was to stand her in good stead in her later years against the mighty following seas of the southern latitudes. Captain Willis insisted on nothing but the best materials, rock elm to the waterline, teak topsides and teak decking, with the result that the builders could not meet the cost and went into bankruptcy, but only after their Scottish craftsmen had produced a magnificent hull. The clipper was moved to Denny's yard where it seems likely that the creditors took over completion of the vessel. By November 1869 the clipper was ready for launching. Captain Jock decided that he would choose a name to make everyone take notice and where else would he look, but in Robert Burns' poem "Tam O'Shanter". Appropriately enough—the figurehead of *The Tweed* was a figure of Burns' hero Tam O'Shanter. Captain Jock obviously had predilection for the works of Robert Burns.

In Burns' poem the inebriated Tam was homeward bound on his old mare Meg when he stumbled on the scene of Hallowe'en revels in progress. Before Tam's astonished gaze, witches and warlocks danced in frenzy to the tune of the pipes played by Old Nick himself.

"But hornpipes, jigs, strathspeys and reels
    Put life and mettle in their heels",
    and, as the bewildered Tam continued to spy,
    "The mirth and fun grew fast and furious,
    The piper loud and louder blew".

Suddenly the beautiful witch Nannie, having cast off most of her clothes except her chemise, made a graceful leap into the air and Tam, who by this time had almost lost his reason, roared out in careless exuberance: "Weel done, Cutty Sark" (Cutty Sark means a short shirt or chemise).

"And in an instant all was dark,
    And scarcely had he Maggie rallied
    When out the hellish legion sallied".

Tam, with Maggie in full gallop, made off down the road with the witches in full pursuit and Nannie in the lead. Maggie leapt over the watercourse, which according to legend is a barrier to witches, but not before Nannie reached out and poor Meg left "her ain grey tail" in Nannie's outstretched hand. From the poem it will be seen how appropriate it was that Captain Jock Willis should choose the name *Cutty Sark* , to follow in the wake of Tam O'Shanter on the bow of *The Tweed*. The figurehead carver Helyer produced a most artistic and beautiful figurehead representing Nannie the witch. Sometimes when the ship was in port a horse's tail was placed in her outstretched hand. On a Monday afternoon, 22nd November, 1869, the gleaming black hull with the two gold strakes leading back from the figurehead and trail boards with their profusion of gold gingerbread work, slipped smoothly down the ways without a hitch. The ship was named by Mrs. Janet Moodie, wife of Captain Moodie who would be appointed master.

The hull was towed to Greenock to receive her masts and rigging. *Cutty Sark* was heavily sparred and spread a greater sail plan than any other ship of the China tea fleet. Her sail plan was designed by John Rennie, chief draughtsman at Scott and Linton.

Cutty Sark was an ideal tea clipper, 212 feet in length, 36 feet in beam, 146 feet from deck to truck, her mainyard was 78 feet and with a full spread of stunsails on both sides, the width of sail extended approximately 156 feet.

Cutty Sark was commanded by Captain G. Moodie, who superintended the building of the ship, and was her master for the first three voyages. Although the new clipper was designed expressly for the China tea trade, she was not fortunate enough to break any records, but she did prove to be a fast racer, her best 24 hour run being 363 sea miles.

The maiden voyage of a ship can be an anxious one for her officers and *Cutty Sark* proved no exception when it became apparent that the ironwork aloft, was beginning to show some weaknesses. Captain Moodie was an excellent seaman—but was compelled to display caution. he did not drive *Cutty Sark* as he would have liked, for repairs had proved necessary. This may be contrasted with Captain Kemble's confidence in *Thermopylae* when he drove her to a record passage on her maiden voyage. However, in spite of the shortcomings of *Cutty Sark*'s ironwork, Captain Moodie discovered that he had a very swift ship and it was under his command that she made one of the fastest day's runs of her career.

Most of the tea clipper fleet carried general cargo to Australia, then picked up a coal cargo for the Chinese ports where they awaited the new season's teas at such places as Canton, Whampoa, Macao, Shanghai and Foo Chow; the last was favoured, because of the early date at which its teas were ready for shipment.

In 1872 *Cutty Sark* left Shanghai, in company with *Thermopylae*. Interest and excitement ran high among the tea clipper crews as this was the chance for *Cutty Sark* to make her reputation as the fastest of the tea clippers by defeating her rival. This was not to be.

Cutty Sark was first away, weighing anchor at 7 p.m. on 17th June. She was held up at the bar by lack of water under her keel and *Thermopylae*, weighing anchor later, crossed the bar close behind her. For some days the two ships were forced to drop anchor in the face of strong headwinds, driving rain and thick fog. On 21st, they dropped their pilots and cleared away to sea. For five days they sailed out of sight of each other until at 1 p.m. near Hong Kong, *Thermopylae* reported *Cutty Sark* several miles ahead. Over the next two days each was alternately in the lead until they parted company. For two weeks *Cutty Sark* did not sight *Thermopylae*, then on 15th July her rival was sighted eight miles away slightly in the lead. At Anjer, Moodie picked up mail while Kemball free of any delay, went straight on through the Sunda Straits. In the open sea *Cutty Sark* was in the lead when a heavy sea breaking under her counter tore away the rudder. Only superb seamanship prevented the disaster of dismasting. The rudder had come clean away and it took six days to make a temporary one, and ship it into place. With the ship pitching in heavy seas, a forge was rigged on the slippery teak deck to fashion the iron work. At one time the forge was overturned, scattering hot coals over the men.

A 70 foot spare spar was cut up to make a jury rudder and post with the ironwork fashioned from iron stantions. On completion the jury rudder was sent overboard and allowed to stream astern at the end of chains. Then by the set of the sails the ship gathered

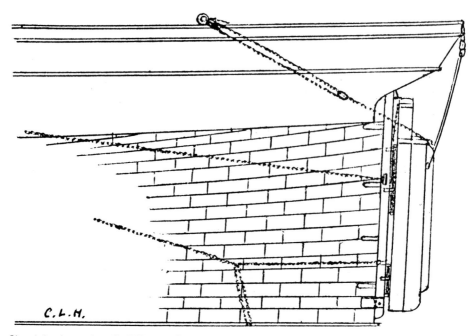

Sketch by the author, Cyril Hume, of the jury rudder used by *Cutty Sark* on her voyage from China to London in 1872.

sternway, the rudder post was hauled into place and the chain guys were led to the wheel. So effective was the repair that after a delay of thirteen days the *Cutty Sark* resumed her voyage and reached London only seven days behind *Thermopylae*.

By 1877 the Suez Canal route had almost eliminated the tea clippers from the China tea trade. Steamers were taking only 42 days by Suez compared with about 100 days by the clippers around the Cape of Good Hope. In that year *Cutty Sark* made her last tea passage.

In the winter of 1877 *Cutty Sark* was lucky to survive a gale in the English Channel in which many lives and ships were lost but not without damage to her bulwarks and the expense of salvaging fees to the tugs who saved her.

In 1878 her master, Captain Tiptaft, died in Shaghai and was succeeded by the mate. Captain Wallace was a genial and popular master and a fine seaman. He was a hard driver and soon had the clipper showing her paces, making some splendid passages. One of her best passages under Captain Tiptaft had been London to Sydney in 1878, taking only 72 days.

A dramatic change in *Cutty Sark's* fortunes took place when she sailed to the east to a notorious "hell ship" voyage. When near Sunda Straits her mate killed a negro seaman in a fight. Captain Wallace placed the mate under close arrest but allowed himself to be connived into letting the mate escape. In spite of the popularity of the Captain, the anger of his incensed crew played on his mind so much that on one calm morning after directing the helmsman's attention to the course, he stepped onto the taffrail and jumped into the Java sea. A boat was quickly lowered but all that could be seen were the sharks swimming furiously around. At Singapore, Captain Bruce was appointed as a new skipper. He was a skilful navigator, reaching a reasonable standard of seamanship in his younger days but by now, was noted as an indifferent seaman and a demon for the bottle when at sea. He brought the first cargo of Indian tea direct from Calcutta to Melbourne, an amount of 83,000 lb. (Australia's annual import from India is now about 60 million pounds). The *Cutty Sark* sailed on to Singapore where cholera struck down many crew members. Two of them died and the rest rejoined the ship weak and emaciated. Australian seaman Henry Horning recounted his return to the *Cutty Sark* as follows:

"When I returned to the *Cutty Sark* I found her still in quarantine. She had been roughly fumigated. I was told that six members of the crew had died and that two were so seriously ill that they would be left behind in hospital. One apprentice was subsequently invalided home, the rest of the crew returned one by one, more like skeletons than living men.

Bruce and Rutland, the mate, immediately ordered the crew to clean the ship for sea with sand and canvas, a back-breaking task for which they were physically unfit. They refused duty, and on the intervention of the port authorities, investigating a complaint by Bruce, the captain was severely censured and the men were ordered a respite from duty. The hell ship voyage continued, and near St. Helena the rations were cut by half.

Cutty Sark obtained some pork from a French ship and later H.M.S. *Thalia* responded to the signal "Short of provisions" by

E

supplying barrels of salt pork and biscuits. The 125 day voyage ended in New York. The second mate demanded an investigation which resulted in the Captain and mate having their certificates suspended.

In spite of his alleged shortcomings Captain Bruce must have had good qualifications as a seaman otherwise he would never have been Captain Fowler's first mate in the *Halloween*.

Henry Horning went to sea for adventure and certainly met more than he bargained for. During a voyage in the *Alice Mary* in 1881, he recorded a typical encounter with pirates. On a voyage to Foo Chow about 100 miles north of Hong Kong, the *Alice Mary* was becalmed about noon, in the midst of a small group of islands. They were immediately surrounded by a large number of junks and it was soon evident that they were pirates. The Captain of the *Alice Mary*, who naturally enough was concerned for his wife who was aboard, decided to put on a "show of force". The armoury which comprised two revolvers, six muzzle-loading muskets and six cutlasses, was brought on deck. Three men with muskets patrolled the starboard side, three the port side. The cutlasses were divided amongst the rest of the crew who took up a stand on the foc's'le deck and amidships. The Captain and mate guarded the poop. It was believed that the pirates, under these circumstances, would not attack before nightfall. But, without this vigilance on the part of the crew the pirates undoubtedly would have swarmed aboard, massacred everybody, looted and burned the ship. The sails slowly filled to an evening breeze and the ship moved away from the screeching pirates. Within one hour the junks were left behind and were hull down to the great relief of all on board the *Alice Mary*.

In another voyage in 1879, he was shipmates with Joseph Conrad, the celebrated sea-writer. He noticed that Conrad spent much time with a black seaman, and it is believed that from that association that Conrad wrote "The Nigger of the Narcissus".

Horning eventually founded a successful real estate business in Sydney, the name of which still exists to this day as H. W. Horning & Co. Pty. Ltd.

Under Captain Moore, *Cutty Sark* carried her first wool cargo from Newcastle to London in 82 days beating her rivals in the wool trade by twenty-five days. Then with another cargo from Newcastle she made the voyage in 79 days. The only clipper to equal her passage was her old rival *Thermopylae*.

In 1885 Jock Willis escorted Captain Richard Woodget to the *Cutty Sark* loading in London for Sydney and brought about a combination that was to make maritime history. The new captain was a most able and efficient seaman and under his command the clipper was to be given the opportunity to see what she could do in the southern latitudes. At last with Willis' approval, Woodget was able to overhaul the rigging to suit his requirements, with orders to report to the Sydney agents, Dangar Gedye and Co. Woodget sailed 931 sea miles in seventy hours followed by a run of 330 sea miles in 24 hours, still close-hauled. *Cutty Sark* arrived in Sydney in 77 days, the fastest passage out. Then came a voyage that was to delight Willis. By way of Cape Horn, Woodget drove the clipper

An early photograph of *Cutty Sark,* probably about 1882. The hull form shows up well and also the muntz metal sheathing.

A special occasion. A photograph taken by Captain Woodget at the break of the poop. Left to right: Miss Jakin and her father from Auckland, N.Z., Miss Holborrow and her mother, Mr. Lipman and his sister. This photograph shows that there was no porch over the companion leading below. Panels on the monkey poop were square and the embellishment on the lifebuoy shows the pride held for that ship.

and made the passage in 73 days, beating her old rival *Thermopylae* by a week.

The next voyage to London was in 72 days against *Thermopylae*'s 87. In 1888, *Cutty Sark* again beat *Thermopylae* with a voyage of 71 days against *Thermopylae*'s 79.

As *Cutty Sark*'s reputation as a fast wool carrier increased she became the last chance for the London Sale, by loading the late arrival wool at the wharfside. She became a great favourite of the Sunday crowds and her crew was lionised and feted. Picnics were organised followed by 'tween deck dances with some of the girls of Sydney.

In her 1889 voyage to Sydney *Cutty Sark* added to her laurels

Captain Woodget of *Cutty Sark,* indulges in his favourite pastime of photographing his visitors and what could be more pleasing for Miss Lipman and Miss Holborrow than standing behind the wheel of the famous clipper.

by passing the P. & O. liner *Britannia,* and beating her into Port Jackson. The clipper was off Gabo Island in light winds when she was passed by the steamer. Twelve hours later the *Britannia* reported the lights of a sailing ship sailing at seventeen knots to their sixteen, the wind being a strong southerly. When *Britannia* entered the Heads at 10 a.m. *Cutty Sark* was at anchor, with sails furled, having arrived two hours earlier.

In 1895, at Brisbane Captain Woodget, screwed in a record 5,304 bales of wool and *Cutty Sark* left the Australian shores for the last time. On arrival in London, Woodget found that Willis had almost completed the sale of the clipper to the new Portuguese owners Ferreira Bros. of Lisbon and was to be renamed *Ferreira,* affectionately known as *El Pequina Camisole.*

In spite of the economies forced on the survivors of the sailing era, the Portuguese owners kept her hull in good condition. After having been blown ashore by a Florida hurricane in 1906, she was refloated to continue her wanderings between Rio, New Orleans and Lisbon.

Cutty Sark, ashore in Florida. She was refloated without any hull damage—a tribute to the shipwrights in Dumbarton, where she was built.

Cutty Sark, at her loading berth, Circular Quay 1886, showing detail of loading ramp with bales of wool awaiting stowage.

A busy day at the quay about 1885. *Cutty Sark,* is alongside the south bank of Circular Quay ready for loading cargo with her yards squared to perfection.

In May 1916, the old clipper, almost completely dismasted in a gale off the Cape of Good Hope, was towed to Capetown and refitted as a barquentine. In spite of the predominance of war news, reports of the clipper were published and the usual crowd of visitors flocked to see her.

There, the usual arguments among the various members of the crews took place; the *Cutty Sark* faction versus the *Thermopylae* faction. One animated discussion became so intense that a *Cutty Sark* advocate induced the opposition to withdraw his viewpoint at the point of his stiletto.

In 1922 she turned up in a London dock, a shabby shadow of her former self and still attracted crowds of visitors. Then a miracle happened in the form of an impetuous gesture on the part of Captain and Mrs, Dowman who purchased her from the Portuguese owners for £3,750. On Captain Dowman's death in 1936,

Mrs. Catherine Dowman presented *Cutty Sark*, along with a capital sum of money for maintenance, to the Incorporated Thames Nautical Training College. In 1938, *Cutty Sark*, in tow, made her last sea voyage from Falmouth to the Thames with the venerable Captain Woodget, at the wheel. By 1949, *Cutty Sark* had outlived her usefulness as a training ship. The famous vessel was offered to the National Maritime Museum, who were without the finances to accept the offer. The London County Council allocated £4,000 for repairs.

His Royal Highness the Duke of Edinburgh, became patron of the Cutty Sark Preservation Society and in a ceremony at Greenwich on 28 May, 1953, *Cutty Sark* was formally handed over to the Duke of Edinburgh. Her Majesty, Queen Elizabeth, accompanied by His Royal Highness the Duke of Edinburgh, officially opened the ship to the public. *Cutty Sark* is now on perpetual exhibition and receives approximately a quarter of a million visitors a year, from many countries of the world.

A model of *Cutty Sark*, made by silversmith Mr. S. J. Sparrow, containing 620 ounces of silver valued in 1975 at £85,000.

Cutty Sark, in Falmouth after restoration by Captain Dowman.

CUTTY SARK "THE FIRST"

CAPTAIN Jock Willis, was not the first ship owner to name *Cutty Sark* for a ship. A little *Cutty Sark* of Hong Kong arrived in Sydney on 30th July, 1867, with Captain Peter Orr, as Master. Captain Peter believed in keeping up appearances for, at the head of his crew list was one, Arrilla of Singapore, whose rank was that of "butler". This little *Cutty Sark* of 474 tons, traded to the Australian ports from Melbourne to Darwin. On 13th August, 1867, she cleared the heads, with nails and 650 tons of Minmi coal for Ningpo, China, sailing into the blue Pacific and obscurity. Many years ago the writer was mystified by a letter from an elderly gentleman who claimed to have visited *Cutty Sark* in Darwin. It seems obvious that the ship in question was the little *Cutty Sark* , "the first". Willis' *Cutty Sark* never visited Darwin.

PATRIARCH

SIXTY eight days to Sydney from London and a new record! With undoubted pride and satisfaction, Captain Pile picked up the pilot off Sydney Heads on 10th February, 1870, and created maritime history. It seemed unbelievable to the news-hungry people of Sydney that they could read London journals published as recently as 4th December, 1869.

The immaculate brand new clipper-ship with the unpretentious name of *Patriarch*, more suggestive of venerability than of speed, with her Aberdeen-green hull, white sparring and delicate tracery of rigging, was the wonder and admiration of the Port of Sydney. The marine reporters were ecstatic. From the press of the day came this quote:—

> "During the last 25 years the port of Sydney and neighbouring colonies have been visited by many clipper ships whose passages from time to time have shown the great advancement that has resulted from the improvement in the art of shipbuilding, but it has fallen to the lot of Captain Pile of the *Patriarch*, which arrived yesterday from London, to totally eclipse anything that has been made between the latter port and Sydney. He has made a passage unprecedented".

Patriarch left the London dock on Tuesday, 30th November, 1869, and proceeded on tour to Greenhithe, where the ship was swung in order to adjust compass.

A slight correction was found to be necessary from the original adjustment at Aberdeen.

The clipper then proceeded to Gravesend where the passengers embarked and live stock was taken on board, followed by departure on the 1st December. The tug was cast off on 2nd December, at Margate, the river pilot leaving the ship at 5 p.m.

Patriarch was off the Isle of Wight at 8 a.m. Friday the 3rd December, where the Channel pilot left the ship and at 6 p.m. the clipper was off the Start.

During an exuberant ceremony of "crossing the line" on November 21st, seaman Albert Bumstead, AB, fell overboard, the two lifebuoys were immediately thrown to him. The ship round-to and the quarter boat was lowered. By this time it was dark and Albert Bumstead was indeed fortunate on being eventually picked up.

The meridian of the Cape was crossed on the 42nd day and in lat. 46° and long. 40E Captain Pile picked up the favourable winds sailing as far south as 59° 35′ and reaching the Cape Pillar, Tasmania, on the 63rd day 6th February, 1870.

Average speed for the previous 19 days 253 knots per day. Off Sydney Heads 10th February with the unbroken record of 69 days for a sailing ship on the London to Sydney route.

The owners of the celebrated Aberdeen-Line of clipper ships were venturesome in that they were always ready to experiment and accept new ideas from their designers, and with remarkably good results.

From the yard of Walter Hood of Aberdeen their first iron ship was launched and her name was *Patriarch*. The beautiful fine lined clipper more than justified their good judgment as demonstrated by her famous maiden voyage. She was built of the best iron plating at a cost of £24,000 which was a good deal of money in those days.

The designers showed great enterprise with the introduction to the spar plan of the unique telescopic masts. The lower and topmasts were of iron in one piece with the topgallant mast of wood, stepped inside the Topmast head. This arrangement eliminated doublings which saved a great deal of weight aloft, and although hard driven *Patriarch* was never dismasted, as so many clippers were and she carried a full suit of stuns'ls into the

'80's. In 1892, *Patriarch* weathered an Indian Ocean Cyclone whereas *Loch Vennacher* 70 miles away was badly dismasted and nearly lost. *Patriarch* during her long career in the Australian trade never had a serious accident. Apparently, the only mishap that could have had serious results happened in the 1874 passage when a heavy gale damaged the wheels and a boat was swept away.

The captain's report did not mention any injury to the helmsman as was a common occurrence under those circumstances when many a seaman suffered broken limbs and other injuries. With the helm out of control there was imminent danger of the ship broaching to, which could mean dismasting and loss of ship. Extract from the Captain's report on reaching Sydney, in 1877:

> "Heavy gale of wind from N.N.W. with high sea. During a sudden lull the ship was struck by a heavy sea which broke 9 ft. off the taffrail and bent 3 stanchion, but luckily doing no other serious damage".

There was a curious happening off the Crozets Islands on 28th June, 1883. As was reported when reaching Sydney:

> "The ship trembled very much from the effects of an earthquake. The shakes lasted 30 minutes and were very severe during the last 10 minutes".

As might be supposed, this was not the effects of a "hangover" on the Captain's part when entering the incident in his log. Similar incidents have been recorded.

The Aberdeen Line took great pride in their ship masters. As seamen they were second to none; of great personality and character, they were well able to cope with their tremendous responsibilities. Captain Pile took *Patriarch* from the stocks and was in command until 1876. Captain Plater then made ten successful voyages, followed by Captain Allan for four voyages. In 1891 Captain Mark Breach took over until the ship was sold.

With these men in command, *Patriarch* became a favourite

Photographed at wheel of *Patriach,* at anchor in Neutral Bay, Sydney; from left to right: Chief Officer Brown, Second Officer Watson, Third Officer Brebner and Captain Mark Breach.

passenger ship. Saturday evening concerts and dancing resulted in expressions of gratitude to the captains and their officers. This was published in the newspapers upon reaching port.

Patriarch was always well manned. On her maiden voyage her crew list included a Bosn's mate, 19 A.B.s, 10 O.S., a butcher, two cooks, 2 stewards and a passenger list of 36 persons. In later years she would have 18 A.B.s and about 6 apprentices.

As a regular wool carrier her passages were always good, and up to 6521 bales could be stowed in her holds.

In stowing wool a good deal depended on the skill of the stevedore both for the safety of the ship and the condition of the cargo on completion of the voyage.

To the Captain fell the responsibility of ensuring that the stevedores screwed in as many bales as possible without straining the deck beams above or the topside planking, and also to ensure that all plank seams were well caulked as the ship would encounter heavy gales and flooded decks on the long eastward passage to Cape Horn. Neglect would cause serious damage to the wool cargo.

The stevedore had to bear in mind the distribution of dead weight cargo which was vital to the trim of the fine-lined clippers to allow the Masters to carry sail for the hard driving ahead.

In loading, the first consideration was the ballasting of the vessel, which in Sydney usually consisted of pigiron, copper ore and sometimes iron bark timber. Care was taken that it was laid parallel to the deck beams above, for the same reason as in a tea cargo so that the bales would fit in evenly without loss of space. On top of the ballast would be laid a layer of loose wood, (termed dunnage) for the purpose of protecting the wrappers of the bales from damage and moisture. This dunnage continued up the sides of the holds as a protection against possible seepage of water through the seams.

In order to make good stowage it was necessary, as each tier was stowed, to insert planks between the bales and with the use of screws varying from six inches to four feet in length the planks were forced apart, the shorter screws being replaced by progressively longer ones, until there was room for another bale.

In the early days of the wool industry several wool ships from Australian ports were lost through the effects of damp wool causing spontaneous combustion. It was believed that shearing sheep in the morning with the previous nights dew on their wool and the wool becoming damp or wet in the drays on the way from the interior were the principal causes.

It was the mate's responsibility to ensure that the wool was free from dampness for the safety of the ship and passengers. This was done by inserting a dry rod into the heart of the bale to test for dampness.

In 1846, through spontaneous combustion a wool cargo smouldered for seventy days. The deck beams of the ship were converted into charcoal, but there were no flames. A similar notable incident was the loss of the Black Ball Line ship *Fiery Star* which sailed from Brisbane in 1865. The Captain and mate, investigating a strong smell coming up from the forecastle, removed the forward hatch and were appalled to find clouds of

An invaluable close up of *Patriach*'s bow showing great detail: plating of the hull, figurehead, trail boards, head boards.

Patriach, the record holder to Sydney (68 days), an iron clipper from Hood's yard in Aberdeen, shows off her telescopic masts (no doubling). These masts were an interesting and successful experiment. During her long career, she was never dismasted.

The loading of wool bales into the forward hatch of *Patriach*.

smoke arising from the lower hold. Every hatch was battened down and the men employed pumping water.

The passengers were obliged to leave their cabins, the smell of the burning wool, which was impregnated with arsenic (used in cleaning it) having become insufferable. Towards evening flames burst out from the bows and deck. The sixty-three passengers were sent off in the boats and the remaining crew made valiant efforts to save the ship. All loose fittings were burnt to keep the fire going under the steam pump. The heat increased until the pitch in the seams began to melt. The crew's efforts were of no avail; finally they were taken off by another ship, *Fiery Star* burnt to the water line and sank.

In Sydney, the season for shipment of wool was from 1st November to 1st March, the principal month being January. The bales varied in weight from two to three and a half and even four cwt. The Average weight was about three cwt. For a cargo of 5,000 bales at one half penny per lb. freight worked out at approximately £3,500. Handling of the bales in the 60's at 4 shillings and 6 pence. per bale would have cost the ship approximately £800 with a cargo of 4,000 bales. Port charges at Sydney in 1864 were: Customs entry and shipping office £4.4.0; Pilotage in, 4 pence per ton, the same out. During the 1890's an enthusiastic and expert amateur photographer Dr. E. Morris Humphery captured deck scenes on board *Patriarch*. One scene shows the screw in operation at the main hatch forcing in the last bales. This is the only known photograph of the men at work with the screw.

On her last passage from Australia, Captain Mark Breach and apprentice Hoare, threw a sealed bottle over the side to test the action of tide and current. 36 years later it was picked up in an Australian river; over that time it had travelled a distance of 100 miles, about 3 miles a year. A somewhat discouraging outlook for castaways of those days, relying on bottle post to be rescued.

In 1897 for the first time in her career, the *Patriarch* failed to get her usual cargo in Sydney and the first class passenger wool clipper was obliged to load coal at Newcastle for Manila. Another blow for Captain Breach, was to find when he reached the

Patriach, under full sail on the port tack clearing Sydney Heads on the long passage with wool for the London market.

A social occasion on board *Patriach*. Captain Mark Breach loved to entertain the pretty girl visitors. Note the elaborate board covering the ends of spare spars.

English Channel that his much loved ship had been sold to the Norwegians for £3,150

For the next dozen years the old Aberdeen flyer tramped around the ports of the globe. In 1903, when bound for Buenos Aires with a cargo of timber she went ashore on the Rio Grande coast, but was refloated and continued her wanderings.

In 1912, on the night of 23rd February while working through the Yucatan Channel, the old ship went ashore on a reef in the Bay of Corrientes, Cuba. A Cuban war vessel went to her assistance, but the ship was hard and fast and beyond salvage, and so ended the career of a magnificent ship.

During her long life, *Patriarch* made many fast passages: Her 1876 passage was a very good one to Sydney of 71 days and in 1884, another good one of 73 days.

In 1885, she reached the equator in 16 days from the "Start" which was phenomenal sailing, arriving at Sydney in 75 days.

Captain Mark Breach on his first voyage in command, drove *Patriarch* to an extraordinary 24 hour run of 377 miles.

Tonnage and dimensions were as follows:

> 1,405 tons Gross, 1,339 tons Net, 221 ft. 1 in. length; 38 ft. 1 in. breadth, 22 ft. 3 ins. depth, freeboard 4 ft. 3½ ins. Her poop of 90 ft. was a record for an iron ship and was a wonderful promenade for her passengers by day, and for dancing in the evening. Underneath the poop there was accommodation for 40 saloon passengers. The cabins were fitted out in a most luxurious and opulent manner, consequently her passenger list was nearly always filled.

As a passenger-ship, cargo and wool carrier, *Patriarch* has fully deserved her place in the annals of maritime history as a splendid example of clipper-ship design at its best.

SALAMIS

O F the great shipping lines that contributed so much to the development of the Australian trade, the Aberdeen Line of sailing ships was second to none. Their green hulls embellished with gold lines, all white sparring and a profusion of polished brass work, made them a familiar sight in the ports around the globe. The celebrated Line dated back to its inception in 1825, by George Thompson Junior. One hundred years later their steamships were still trading along the old sea routes.

Officially, the name was "Aberdeen Line" which became generally known as the "Aberdeen White Star Line", probably because of the insignia of an 8-point white star predominant in carvings around the hull and the 8-point white star of the house-flag. (As stated elsewhere, the 8-point star was changed to 6 points on the house flag in 1879, possibly to make it more discernable at a distance).

The speedy little *Phonecian* an early Aberdeen Line ship, is believed to have carried the first shipment of gold, valued at £81,000, from Melbourne to England in 1852.

Their first clipper ships almost dominated the tea, gold, wool and passenger trade. They were nearly all designed and built by Hood of Aberdeen, the notable exceptions were the *Thermopylae* and *Salamis* (each built to the same design). Their designer was Bernard Waymouth, Naval Architect, later Secretary to Lloyd's of London.

The last sailing ship of the Line was the 3-mast steel barque *Strathdon* 2093 tons, built by Harland and Wolff of Belfast, Ireland in 1885. *Strathdon* was acquired by the Aberdeen Line in 1890, when her first name *Queen's Island* was changed.

The beautiful iron clipper *Salamis*, in a Melbourne dry dock. A little larger than *Thermopylae*, and built on the same lines, with many fast passages to her credit.

Strathdon was sold to the French Line of A. D. Bordes in 1905, into the nitrate trade and renamed *Gers*. Having outlived her usefulness she was finally broken up in 1924.

There were no fewer than 59 sailing ships owned by the Aberdeen Line during the years 1825 to 1890. They were of wood and composite construction, nine iron clippers and one steel barque.

In the later years of the 19th century, economies were forced on their sailing ships as was applied to all sailing ships at that time, sometimes to the extreme. One old Master recorded that all surplus fat was saved from the galley, barrelled and resold in Aberdeen. The same Master declared that the seagulls were somewhat wary of the ships from Aberdeen with so little thrown over the side that it became necessary for the gulls to carry a "cut lunch" under their wings. Be that as it may, the construction of their clipper ships reached the pinnacle of perfection regarding speed and beauty of form.

Of all the iron clippers of the wool fleet the favourite of the seaman of those days appeared to be the *Salamis*. The famous Captain Holmes, a well-known master in the wool trade, said this of her: "Above all considerations and from among all the ships that I have known, the *Salamis* remains the loveliest thing in my memory". Praise indeed! Designed on the same lines as *Thermopylae*, as a racing tea clipper, she was only slightly larger to give a tonnage of 1021 tons, as compared to *Thermopylae*'s 948 tons, with an increase on the spar plan. She gained herself a reputation for being the fastest iron clipper of the Australian wool fleet. Built in 1875, at the yard of Walter Hood of Aberdeen as were most of the Aberdeen Line of clippers, *Salamis* was 212 ft. 6 ins. in length, with a breadth of 36 ft. and a depth 21 ft. 7 inches. her sparring was considered to be large enough for a ship of 1500 tons. The new clipper was intended for the same trade as *Thermopylae*, general cargo to Melbourne, Australian coal to China and then the new season's teas for the London markets. But unfortunately for the *Salamis* the tea steamers were too well established after seven years of trading through the Suez Canal and the clipper was quite unable to obtain a tea cargo. She was

Discharge of R. B. McKilliam, Second Mate of the *Thermopylae*, reproduced courtesy of his son, Mr. R. L. McKilliam of Sydney. R. B. McKilliam was later First Mate of the *Samuel Plimsoll* and his first command was of the sailing ship *Salamis*, he also commanded several steamships including the S.S. *Salamis*. Captain McKilliam died in 1934 at the age of 73.

swift and beautiful, but built too late to achieve fame as a tea clipper. As were the regular tea clippers, *Salamis* was channelled into the Australian wool trade and it was there that she became a celebrity. Her passages to Melbourne were never equalled by any other iron clipper. Over 13 passages the clipper averaged 75 days from pilot to pilot. Under Captain McKilliam she reached a speed of 19 knots. With the skipper below, the mate reported to him that the clipper was flying through the water at a terrific speed. Captain McKilliam went on deck and checked the log with the mate and sure enough, for a short burst of speed, it was logged at 19 knots. Rising seas then compelled the Captain to take in sail.

On one passage *Salamis* experienced the dangers of the westerly gales when a heavy sea came up from astern, smashed the wheel, washed the helmsman into the mizzen rigging, broke the cabin skylight flooding the cabin and carried away the binnacle and the compass.

From 1875 to 1894 *Salamis* had only two masters, Captain Phillip Senior and Captain Phillip Junior. Both were eminently successful and between them built up her reputation which was maintained by Captain R. B. V. McKilliam, ex-2nd mate of *Thermopylae* and 1st mate of *Samuel Plimsoll* who had the kind of experience that frequently gave *Salamis* the best passage of the season. *Salamis* was not fitted for passengers and was designed purely as a racing cargo ship. Her wool cargo was in the vicinity of 5,500 bales.

Her Melbourne trade came to an end in 1899, when she was sold to L. Gunderson of Porsgrund, Norway and reduced to barque rig. Like her sisters of the wool fleet she was reduced to tramping and with ignominious cargoes of guano. In May 1905, she was anchored off Malden Island in mid Pacific when a gale sprang up overnight. She was driven ashore and became a complete loss, the wreck being sold for a nominal 5 shillings; a sad ending for the beautiful green and gold hulled ship with her magnificent sparring soaring up 150 feet from the deck.

SAMUEL PLIMSOLL

IN 1873, there was launched from the Hood shipbuilding yard in Aberdeen an iron clipper for George Thompson's Aberdeen Line. This was the third iron clipper following the highly successful *Patriarch* and *Militiades* for George Thompson who named his new ship after the Parliamentarian, Samuel Plimsoll.

By a strange twist of fate, that which is known as the Plimsoll Mark, on a ship's topside, could be justly called the Hallmark. In 1854, James Hall with his brother, founded a shipping line which they ran efficiently, gaining experience over the years with ship's cargoes and crews. Hall was very conscious of the deplorable conditions on the ships that put to sea, and it was he who first proposed the idea that there should be rigid restrictions on the weight of cargo carried. Unscrupulous ship owners were sending ships to sea in an unseaworthy state knowing that there was litle chance of survival for ship and crew, thereby collecting the insurance.

Hall declared that the freeboard of a ship should not be less than 3 ft. to 5 ft. according to the size of the vessel. Although Lloyd's had a rule to that effect it was seldom adhered to.

Samuel Plimsoll M.P. for Derby listened to a speech by Hall and realised that this was a cause which gave him an opportunity of making himself heard in the House of Commons, where he was unknown and unnoticed. Hall gave him all the necesary details of his proposed load line of safety.

With tremendous enthusiasm and dedication to his task Plimsoll year after year assailed the Commons with his proposals. It was not until 1875, that he won his case—the Government

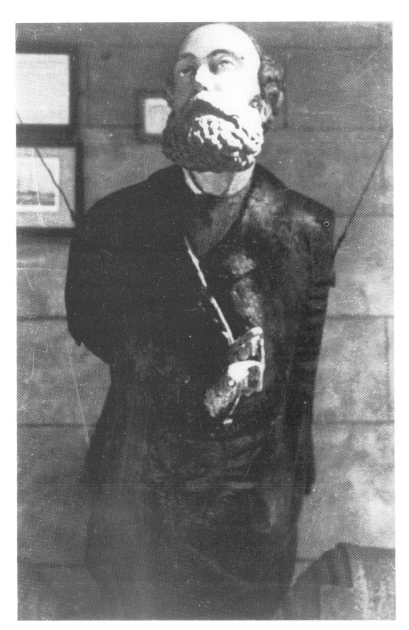

The figurehead of *Samuel Plimsoll*.

made a load line obligatory. He had published a book in 1873, that caused tremendous interest especially among the working classes in sympathy with the lot of the seaman. It was Plimsoll's persistent rhetoric in the house that finally won the day.

Hall's participation became forgotten and Samuel Plimsoll was given full credit for the innovation. Hall was the unsung hero and to him should go the credit for a most necessary reform. In a letter to Hall in 1890, Bernard Weymouth of Lloyd's wrote: "I know full well that it is to you that all honour is due for the steps you took to stop the overloading of ships and to prevent unseaworthy ships from proceeding to sea. Plimsoll traded on your brains".

Nevertheless, it was the combined efforts of both men that led to the saving of many lives and ships. However, Plimsoll did force the issue and is remembered.

Plimsoll visited Australia in 1882. He and his wife stayed at Melbourne and Sydney but, at Brisbane, unfortunately, his wife died of pneumonia.

The *Samuel Plimsoll* with its figurehead carved in his likeness, like George Thompson's earlier iron ships, was specially fitted for passengers and migrants to Australia, and invariably carried wool on the return passage. For her first fifteen years, she sailed to Sydney and was then diverted to the Melbourne trade.

In 1875, the clipper came into collision with an Italian barque *Eurica* which sank. The crew was rescued and put ashore at Falmouth. There was little damage to the sturdy iron hull of the *Samuel Plimsoll*.

On the 1879 passage to Australia, when nearing the Equator, *Samuel Plimsoll* was struck by a sudden, violent storm, a squall from the southward. The bobstay carried away. This stay sometimes consisted of an iron bar or a heavy duty chain, led from the end of the bowsprit to the stem of the hull nearer the waterline and was regarded by seamen as the most important stay on the ship. It was the foundation of the fore and aft stays of all the masts and with the failure of this stay there was nothing to support them and that meant a total collapse of jibboom, fore topmast and all the upper spars over the side in a tremendous tangle of gear. The effect on the master of a ship under these

The well known clipper ship *Samuel Plimsoll*, which led such an adventurous life.

Samuel Plimsoll, dismasted.

circumstances must have been appalling, especially as the safety of the passengers and the crew was on his shoulders. The potential loss of his ship, his duty towards the owners, called for the highest level of seamanship.

Captain Bowden, anxious to avoid the tremendous expense of making for the nearest port under jury rig, set to work with his crew, salvaged all the gear back on to the deck. The formidable task was then to replace the broken-off portion of the bowsprit into its original position which was affected by means of timber projections driven into the stump. All spars were sent aloft and re-rigged in turbulent seas. After a delay of seventeen days the *Samuel Plimsoll* was again on her course. A magnificent exhibition of seamanship at its best; no doubt much appreciated by the owners and underwriters!

Pillar Box steering gear photographed on *Excelsior*, the same type that was fitted to *Samuel Plimsoll* and *Thermopylae*.

HAWKESBURY

OF the great passenger and wool carrying ships, few were better known than the *Hawkesbury*. As a member of a syndicate, Mr. F. H. Dangar of Sydney was associated with Devett and Moore in the building of this fine vessel. Letters covering the transaction are still in existence and it is interesting to note the financial aspect. At an estimated cost of £19,000, four payments to the builders were required of £4,750 each. The first falling due after the framing of vessel was completed viz. 15th September, 1868; the second after launch viz. 1st March, 1869, the third 6 months later viz. 1st September, 1869 and the final payment on delivery 1st October, 1869.

A most interesting sidelight in these letters was the discussion re the naming of the new ship. *Earl of Belmore* and *Royal Visitor* were submitted as appropriate names to Devett & Moore, the former in honour of the Governor of the day, and the latter possibly to commemorate the visit of the Duke of Edinburgh.

To quote Devett & Moore's reply:—

> With reference to your suggestions as to a name, there is already a large American built ship called the *Royal Visitor*, moreover we have a strong objection to any **personal** names. A public man may at anytime with or without just cause become unpopular, and there are also two sets of opinions about most public characters. The suggestion most approved on this side is to call her the *Hawkesbury*. It is a colonial name, and is following up the same idea as the *Parramatta*, thus readily identifying the new ship as belonging to the same line, which we consider an advantage.

In the above painting of *Cutty Sark*, her rival the *Thermopylae*, can be seen in the distance. The other painting on this page features Thermopylae, with a distant *Cutty Sark*. Both paintings depict these ships in their original clipper rig, as they were in 1872, on the only occasion that they raced each other from China to London.

(Paintings by Malcolm C. Armstrong).

FLAGS

Cutty Sark's signal letters

were J K W S.
This is how they appeared when hoisted using the Commercial Code of Signals in use at that time.

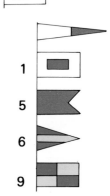

J

K

W

S

Thermopylae's signal letters W P V J

are shown below on the left.

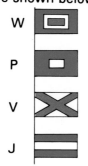

W

P

V

J

Prior to 1869, Marryat's Universal Code of Signals was in use and *Thermopylae's* signal flags were then 1 5 6 9, under the Fourth Distinguishing Pendant, as shown here on the right:

1

5

6

9

In Marryat's code there were only 17 flags and pendants, They were usually made very large 6 ft.× 8 ft., and the pendants 4 ft.× 18 ft.

HOUSE FLAGS

Thompson's Aberdeen Line
Owner of 22 ships in 1877 including *Thermopylae*. Note, in 1879 the 8 pointed star on the house flag was changed to a 6 pointed star.

John Wills & Son
Owner of 15 ships in 1877 including *Cutty Sark*

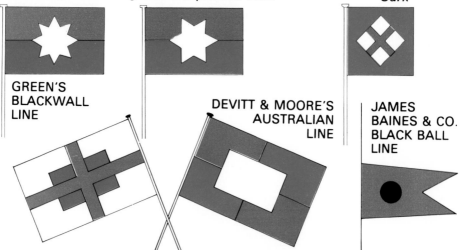

GREEN'S
BLACKWALL
LINE

DEVITT & MOORE'S
AUSTRALIAN
LINE

JAMES
BAINES & CO.
BLACK BALL
LINE

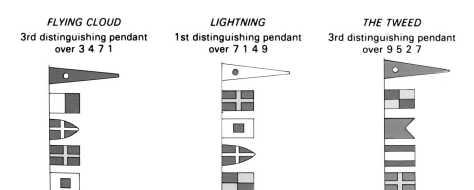

FLYING CLOUD	LIGHTNING	THE TWEED
3rd distinguishing pendant over 3 4 7 1	1st distinguishing pendant over 7 1 4 9	3rd distinguishing pendant over 9 5 2 7

The above flags are from Marryat's Universal Code of Signals.

FLYING CLOUD was built by Donald McKay of Boston for American owners in 1851 and was later sold to the English Black Ball Line of J. BAINES.

LIGHTNING was built by Donald McKay in 1854 for J. Baines & Co. for the Australian run. On her maiden voyage from Boston to Liverpool she set a world record for a sailing ship of 436 miles in 24 hours.

THE TWEED was built at the Bombay dockyard in 1854.

CARLISLE CASTLE was built in Glasgow in 1868 for Green's Blackwall Line. She was in the Australian passenger and wool trade for 30 years and was finally lost with all hands on the West coast of Australia. Below on the left are her signal letters by Marryat's Code, comprising 4th distinguishing pendant over 1 7 6 4. On the right are her later signal letters according to the Commercial Code of Signals, H J F G.

MACQUARIE ex MELBOURNE

The last ship to be owned by Green's she was later owned by Devitt & Moore. Her signal letters were P C G L (Commercial Code of Signals) as shown on the right.

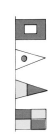

Painting of *Cutty Sark*, by David Hogan. *Cutty Sark*'s sails were reduced in 1880 and, as shown in this painting, she no longer had a sky sail.

This model of the *Cutty Sark*, was made by the author and is now in the Sydney Museum of Applied Arts and Sciences. It was Cyril Hume's first model. It was his research into the life and construction of *Cutty Sark*, when making this model, that led to a lifetime study of sailing ships and the men who sailed in them.

On Saturday morning, 25th July, 1889, the new P. & O. liner *Britannia*, left Melbourne for Sydney. Six hours later the *Cutty Sark*, departed. On Sunday afternoon, a Southerly Buster hit the coast off Gabo Island. During the evening—it was a clear moonlight night, officers on the bridge of the *Britannia*, observed lights in the distance astern. It was the *Cutty Sark*. To the delight of the passegers lining the rails of the liner, the *Cutty Sark*, swept past. On the Monday morning when the *Britannia* entered Sydney harbour, the *Cutty Sark*, was already at anchor with sails furled. A triumph for sail over steam.

(Painting by David Hogan).

Model of *Thermopylae*, by the author. Cyril Hume estimated that he put 8,000 hours of work into the making of this model. Not that he considered it **work** in the usual sense of the word, but he took meticulous care with accuracy and detail, and acquired an astounding knowledge and love of ships and seamen.

A model of Cutty Sark's figurehead, made by the author. The figurehead is Nannie the witch, from Robert Burns' poem Tam O'Shanter. In the poem, Nannie held a mare's tail in her hand, and when *Cutty Sark*, was in port, the mare's tail was sometimes improvised from rope yarn. In Cyril Hume's model, the "mare's tail", was donated by his neighbour's cat.

On Christmas Eve, 1893, *Cutty Sark*, left Sydney, for the last time. The pilot steamer is *Captain Cook II*, which came into service only a few months before this occasion.

(Painting by Malcolm C. Armstrong).

This was the second of three Sydney pilot steamers, to bear the name *Captain Cook*. She was in service from 1893, until 1939. During the second world war she was used as a sea cadet training vessel in Sydney harbour and she was scuttled in 1947. She and her successor, were built with a hull like that of a sailing ship, including clipper bow. Originally, she had two masts (as shown in the painting, by Malcolm Armstrong with *Cutty Sark*, on opposite page), and could be sailed as a schooner, and her bridge was abaft the funnel. She underwent structural changes, and this painting shows how she appeared in later life. Many ship lovers now wish she had been restored, but unfortunately neither she nor *Captain Cook III*, is any longer afloat.

Painting by Oswald Brett, now in the possession of Mr. and Mrs. John Kenny; photo courtesy John Frizzel, Esq.

Painting of the barque *Manga Reva*, being met by the tug *Daniel McAllister*, in the misty approaches to New York; by Oswald Brett. A four masted steel barque, she was built at Glasgow in 1891. as the *Pyrenees*. When bound from Tacoma to Leith in 1900, her grain cargo caught fire and she was beached at Manga Reva Atoll. In 1902, she was salved, towed first to Tahiti and then to San Francisco, for rebuilding under a new name acquired from the atoll on which she was beached. In 1914, she was taken over by James P. McAllister in partnership with R. W. Geiske, and they ran her until she was torpedoed by a U-Boat in 1917

(Painting reproduced courtesy McAlister Brothers Inc., New York).

Painting "The lonely sea and sky", by Malcolm C. Armstrong. The ship is the *Marco Polo*, which in 1852, under the command of Captain "Bully" Forbes, sailed from Liverpool to Melbourne, in a record 68 days and completed the round trip in less than 6 months.

Painting of the *Samuel Plimsoll*, by Jack Spurling, who died in 1933. This painting and the five other Spurling paintings which are reproduced in this book, were first published by the Blue Peter Publishing Company Ltd., of London ˙and appeared in the Book *Sail*, volumes one and two, published in 1927 and 1929 respectively.

Painting of *The Tweed*, by Jack Spurling. *The Tweed*, was well known as the flag ship of John Willis who bought her in 1862, gave her this name, and gave her a figurehead representing Tam O'Shanter. It is perhaps not so well known that she was built in Bombay, as a ten gun frigate for the Indian Marine. Her original name was *Punjab*, and she had engines and two paddle wheels. When the Indian Marine merged with the Royal Navy, the ship was sold, her engines were taken out and the guns were used as ballast.

Painting of the *MacQuarie*, by Jack Spurling. Best known as a passenger ship in the Australian trade, *MacQuarie* was built for comfort, not for speed. Built for Green's Blackwall Line, as the *Melbourne*, in 1875, she was bought by Devitt and Moore, in 1887 and her name was changed the following year. From 1904, until 1909, she carried timber for Norwegian owners and bore the name *Fortuna*. She then became a coal hulk in Sydney.

Painting of the *Red Jacket*, by Jack Spurling. This was another well known passenger ship, carrying immigrants from Britain to Australia, from 1854 until 1869. She was American owned and built and was a great rival of the *Lightning*. Her figurehead was a portrait of an Indian Chief.

Painting of *Taeping*, by Jack Spurling. *Taeping*, was launched in 1863 at Greenock, two years before the launching of *Ariel*. The two names are closely associated because of their exciting race in 1866. There were five ships that finished within two days of each other on that occasion. Usually there was only one winner in the race from China and it was worth a healthy bonus to captain and crew, of the first ship home. In sight of each other in the English Channel, *Taeping*, was a mile astern when *Ariel*, picked up the pilot, but *Taeping*, docked 20 minutes ahead of her rival. The ships made a race of it right to the last minute, but unbeknown to them, their owners could not bear it and agreed to share the winners's premuim, to avoid any dispute about which ship was the winner.

Painting of *Sir Lancelot*, by Jack Spurling. A sister ship of the *Ariel*, and launched in the same year. She was built specifically for the China tea trade and her best passage from China to London, was a record 89 days in 1869. During one 24 hour period on that voyage, she sailed 354 miles. she was sold in 1895, and was lost with all hands, in that year in bad weather off the mouth of the Hooghly.

The restored *Cutty Sark*, in her resting place at Greenwich. This, and the other photographs of the *Cutty Sark*, taken at Greenwich and reproduced in this book, were taken by the author, Cyril Hume, when he visited the ship in 1973.

Dumbarton, photographed in 1973 by Cyril Hume, birthplace of the *Cutty Sark*, 104 years previously.

The lady at the wheel of the *Cutty Sark*, is Doreen Walsh, a friend of the author who assisted with compiling the original manuscript for this book.

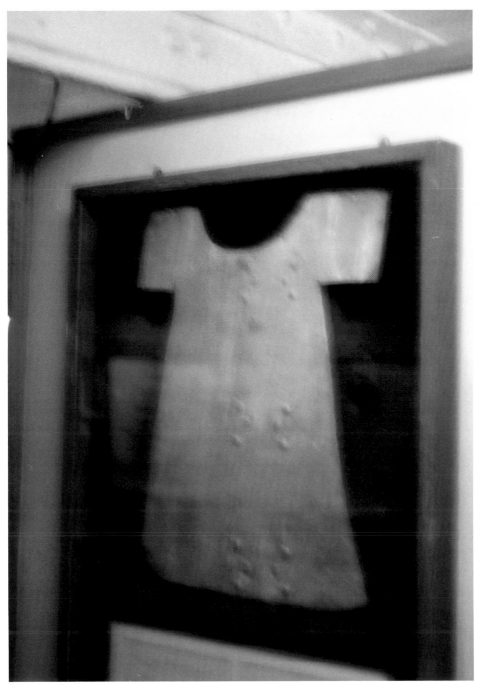

The *Cutty Sark*'s emblem, now on permanent display on the ship. In Robert Burn's poem, Nannie the witch, was wearing a cutty sark or short shirt. The emblem is made of metal, and was worn at the mainmasthead, when *Cutty Sark*, was in port.

Two views of the masts and rigging of the *Cutty Sark*, at Greenwich.

Two paintings of the clipper *Halloween*, by Malcolm C. Armstrong. One of the author's favourite ships. On a voyage from England to Sydney in 1873, the *Halloween*, was struck by a violent squall, which carried away her bowsprit, foretopmast and main topgallant mast. Four days later, masts and rigging had been restored and she was all shipshape again—a remarkable example of seamanship by Captain Watt and his crew. *Halloween*, took 84 days for the voyage to Sydney. On her return passage from China to London in 1873, she equalled Sir Lancelot's record of 89 days.

Painting of the *Flying Cloud*, by the author, Cyril Hume. One of the fastest of the American clippers, *Flying Cloud*, twice made the voyage from New York, to San Francisco, in a record 89 days. She came to an end in 1874, when gutted by fire in St John, N.B.

Painting of the *Lightning*, by Cyril Hume. *Lightning*, was a very fast ship. She made many voyages with passengers from England to Australia, and held the record of 64 days from Melbourne to Liverpool. She is another ship that fell victim to fire. Her cargo of wool caught fire at the wharf in Geelong in 1869, and she could not be saved.

Built to the model of the *South Australian* which Devett & Moore considered to be the best fitted vessel they had seen at that time, the *Hawkesbury*, of composite construction, was built by Pile of Sunderland, and her constructional details fully bore out the prestige of her builders. The vessel was fitted with all the latest appliances for the proper facility for working ship, and the saloon was considered to be equal to that of any vessel afloat. Her dimensions were 1120 reg. tonnage, 203 ft. length, 36·2 ft. beam, 21·5 ft. depth with an extensive poop of 74 ft. and foc's'cle deck of 36 ft.

The *Hawkesbury* was delivered before the specified time as she was launched in November 1868, and leaving Plymouth on 23rd February, arrived in Sydney on the completion of her maiden voyage 19th May, 1869, after a good passage of 85 days. She was commanded by Captain Sayers who was long and favourably known in the Sydney trade. The *Hawkesbury* possessed admirable sailing qualities, having made during this voyage 14½ knots.

In 1874, *Hawkesbury* sailed from Sydney for Foo Chow for a tea cargo but most of her life was on the London-Sydney trade. Her passages were always good although she acquired a reputation as the worst ship in the wool fleet for taking heavy seas aboard, nevertheless she always had a full passenger list. *Hawkesbury* passed into Swedish ownership in 1889, and in 1901, was sold to Captain G. Moltedo, an Italian ship master who also commanded her. Her name was changed to *Pinin*, registered at Genoa.

In 1904, *Pinin* ran ashore in the treacherous Goodwin Sands. Tremendous seas were running with blinding snow squalls, but the London tug *Hibernia* got a line on board and with the assistance of Deal boatmen succeeded in towing the *Pinin* to a safe anchorage.

The fine old ship which had served the Australian trade so well was finally sold to the shipbreakers at Dunkirk and broken up in 1905.

G

GLADSTONE

THE first ship owned by Dangar, Gedys & Co. was the *Gladstone*, named after the British Prime Minister, with whom F. H. Dangar had a close personal friendship. She was. built by McMillan of Dumbarton, and launched as the *Francisco Calderon*, after a one-time president of Peru.

Although termed a "coolie ship", the real purpose was the slave trade, and, at the time of her launch, the traffic in Chinese slaves for the Peruvian and Chilean Islands was at its height. It was when this trade was declared illegal as the result of British intervention, that the ship was sold to Dangar, Gedys & Co. in May, 1875.

When she arrived in Sydney two tons of leg irons and handcuffs were found in the ballast and each bulwark stanchion was fitted with a ring bolt for the chaining of slaves.

Gladstone was launched in 1874, as an iron screw barque, 818 registered tonnage, 248·2 ft. length, 34·2 ft. beam and 20·9 ft. depth of hold, poop 57 ft. foc's'cle 33 ft. Engines were compound, generating 100 h.p. driving a 2 bladed screw at eight knots, under sail as well, thirteen knots. The propeller shaft, fitted with a universal joint and working in a tunnel, could be operated to lift the screw out of water.

Gladstone was converted to ship rig, with skysails above the royals, and with a graceful sheer, nicely turned bow and stern, her appearance would please any nautical eye. The engines were sold to the A.S.N. Co., and used in the steamship *Egmont*.

Under the Dangar Gedys flag, *Gladstone*'s first voyage was to Shanghai with 1,410 tons of Wollongong coal, which filled her to the lower deck beams. She was commanded for many years by

Captain Jackson, who on retiring from the sea was appointed Collector of Tonnage Dues and Manager of Government Wharves until the inception of the Sydney Harbour Trust. Captain Jackson was a practical man, and, with a mind to improve the facilities of the Port, expounded the idea of transforming Farm Cove into another Woolloomooloo Bay. But this idea, fortunately, was even too much for the foreshore despoilers of the day.

Of many extraordinary yarns of the sea, one of the strangest concerns the *Gladstone* while running her easting down on a voyage from London to Sydney. With a breeze on her port quarter and everything set and ship rolling, one of the crew was standing on the pinrail bucketing up water into a tub for washing decks. the ship rolled to windward and back, the mizzen staysail sheet lifted under the sailor's heels and tipped him overboard, where he managed to draw his sheath knife, rip his leg boots down the side and kick them off. An albatross had been following the ship for

Dangar's *Gladstone*, in the Thames during the 70's, by photographer Gould whose magnificent work captured many famous emigrants at the same spot.

some time and mistaking the man for refuse, swooped down. The seaman grabbed the bird around the beak and held its head under water until it drowned, using the buoyancy of the bird's body to support himself. Meanwhile, on board ship an apprentice was sent aloft to keep sight of the man and a boat was launched under difficulties, being sent away with Chief Officer Rugg to effect the rescue. The seaman, one of that hardy race of seafarers, the Norwegians, would in later years display the scars on his hands to verify his story.

Count Von Luckner, the German raider of World War 1, liked the story, and performed another act of piracy by including it in his autobiography with himself as the hero.

Gladstone, after many successful years in the Australian trade, passed into Italian ownership in 1907, and was scrapped at Genoa in 1910.

On board the *Gladstone*, Captain John Jackson on the left with his First Mate Smith from Hobart, Second Mate Andrew Logan of Glasgow and a visitor Livingston Mann. (No record of the dog's name).

NEOTSFIELD

THE people of Sydney love the spectacular, especially on the harbour front, and turn out in their many thousands to such events as the arrival and departure of the sailing training ships, *Esmeralda*, *Libertad* and *Dewarutji*, the start of a Sydney-Hobart yacht race, or an excited armada of small craft jostling Sir Francis Chichester and *Gipsy Moth IV*, when the surface of the usually calm waters of Port Jackson is churned into foam by the somewhat over enthusiastic spectator fleet. How could it be otherwise with the ever growing numbers from the "small fry" upwards, who soak themselves in the thrills and adventures of the salt water sports?

At the end of the Nineteenth Century, the spectator crowds gathered at Circular Quay at lunch time and at weekends to admire and talk about their favourites of the wool clipper fleet. One in particular, provided a proprietary interest because she was Sydney owned, as tall, graceful and well-found as any ship that ever graced east side or west side Circular Quay. Her name was *Neotsfield*.

Built to the order of F. H. Dangar of Dangar, Gedys & Co., Sydney, by Messrs. A. McMillan & Sons of Dumbarton on the Clyde, shipbuilders, who were responsible for as fine a fleet of sailing ships as any shipbuilding firm in the United Kingdom. In design she was not an extreme clipper in any way, but a good carrier and a fine sailer for her day. She had to be, to compete in the annual race for the London wool sales with those greyhounds of the sea, *Thermopylae* and *Cutty Sark* hard on her heels.

Launched August 10, 1889, of 1894 registered tonnage, her dimensions were: length 269 ft. 6 ins.; breadth 40 ft. 1 in.; depth of hold 22 ft. 7 ins.; poop 44 ft. long; foc's'cle deck 28 feet and could stow 3,000 tons of cargo.

Heavily sparred without being overhatted , she crossed double t'gallant yards on fore and main, with graceful poles to each masthead, and proved to be what she looked, a well proportioned powerful ship, able to tear through the combers of the roaring forties, and yet fine enough to give a good account of herself in light weather.

Her hull, with painted ports, Navy fashion, combined with a pleasing sheer rising to the figurehead and spike boom, decks kept in yachtlike order brought much admiration and obviously it was nothing but the best for F. H. Dangar. He was responsible also for the considerable sacrifice of carrying capacity to ensure that the ship would be a worthy representative in the "Golden Fleece Derby" and that is just what she proved to be.

At this stage, the spike bowsprit or spike boom was being widely adopted by ship builders for their steel ships. Up to 22 inches in diameter at the bed, 50 feet or more in length, constructed of rolled steel plating gammoned down with a steel band with double bobstays and guys, it well fulfilled its function of being the most important spar on the ship.

Originally, in the Sixteenth century, the sprit was a single spar steeved at a high angle. Then in the Seventeenth century, a spritboom was added to the outer end. Then as ship design improved, apple bows gave way to fine-lines. Ships were required to sail more to windward culminating in the wonderful perform-ances of the tea clippers with their spectacular array of headsails, foretopmast staysail, inner jib, outer jib, flying jib and jib topsail or jib o' jib. To cope with this arrangement the jibboom was placed along the top of the bowsprit with an extension for the flying jib with a further extension for the jib o' jibboom. This was later modified to one long spar, over the bowsprit, up to seventy feet in length. The chief mates of the clippers would take a keen delight in taking up the martingales so that they could effect an exaggerated steeve downwards. As harbour moorings and whar-fage become more congested, regulations were introduced requiring ships to rig their jibbooms in, but the spike boom, eliminated the necessity for this.

Neotsfield usually berthed at Circular Quay in the south-east corner with other world famous aristocrats of the wool fleet berthed along each side of the Quay. The southern shore by the late Eighties was occupied by the ferry wharves to cater for the needs of the rapidly expanding city of Sydney.

F. H. Dangar was a keen and successful businessman, but he also had an eye for a fine ship. He spared no expense on the fitting out of *Neotsfield* which was evident in the unusually spacious and comfortable accommodation provided for the officers and crew, who, apparently, were the envy of the port. The petty officers had a spacious deckhouse abaft the foremast and the eight apprentices lived in style in the Liverpool house, abaft the mainmast, with curtains fitted on brass rods to the front of their bunks.

The *Neotsfield*, on Christmas Day. Note the Christmas bushes on yard arms and no doubt there is a Christmas message in the flag signals.

The *Neotsfield*, under sail. She was owned by the Sydney firm of F. H. Dangar, and was sunk during the First World War.

The quarters aft for the Master, officers and passengers were smart and comfortable, with well appointed staterooms around the elliptical stern and centrally situated was an elaborately fitted saloon, provided with a horseshoe shaped dining table and revolving chairs upholstered in silk plush. The whole of the furnishing scheme was carried out in bird's eye maple and Nyassawood panelling.

The hand-rails and the brackets were mounted with electroplate, and in the fore part of the saloon was a large marble-top sideboard, surmounted by electroplate guards, and at the back a large plate-glass mirror in ornamental frame. Electric bells communicated from the cabins to the saloon, and there were baths for passengers and for officers. The four two-berth staterooms were off the saloon, two on either side, and very roomy and well furnished, each with a settee and patent lavatory and toilet fittings. The ventilation was all that could be wished—a large port to each stateroom in addition to the air spaces above the bulkhead. The captain's apartment was exceedingly well furnished and spacious. There was a grand promenade on the poop, and a chart-room, which for furnishing could hold its own with any similar place in any of the large mail steamers. The place was upholstered like the saloon, in silk plush, with the panelling in teak and oak.

Chief Officer Rugg, formerly of the *Gladstone*, was appointed to command *Neotsfield* and superintend her building. Her maiden voyage was a good one, at times logging 310 sea miles, with a cargo of 4,000 tons and was off Wilson's Promontory 76 days out. *Neotsfield* continued her career in the Sydney wool trade, maintaining a good and steady average. In 1901, she had the distinction of being the first ship floated into the newly completed Mort's Dock at Woolwich.

The end of the wool carrying era for sailing ships was near by 1902, and *Neotsfield* was sold for £10,000 into the West Coast of South America nitrate trade in competition with the great German nitrate clippers *Preussen* and *Potosi*. *Preussen* was the only five mast square rigger ever built, crossing yards on all five masts and set 30 square sails and eighteen fore and afters.

Neotsfield kept clear of accident, but in the early part of World War I, arrived at Plymouth after a severe storm battering, having lost her bulwarks and figurehead.

Her end came on 17th June, 1917, when 112 miles south-west-by-south from Bishop's Rock, she was stopped by a German submarine. The crew were allowed to leave by their boats, time bombs were set and the fine old fullrigger took her final plunge to the bottom.

The firm of Dangar, Gedy & Co. (later to be known as Dangar, Gedy and Malloch) acted as agent for such celebrated ships as *The Tweed, Hawkesbury, Hallowe'en* and, of course, *Cutty Sark*. In 1891, this firm shared with *Cutty Sark* the honour of a record loading: 4,638 bales of wool, besides other cargo, below hatches, in eight working days. The arrival of *Neotsfield* was an event of major importance to the Sydney shipping reporters because she was a Sydney owned wool carrier. Therefore, the ship received a fine description which is quoted in part:—

"SYDNEY MORNING HERALD   "7th January, 1890
ARRIVAL OF THE NEOTSFIELD MAGNIFICENT
SPECIMEN OF A SYDNEY-OWNED SHIP.

Without doubt as beautifully modelled and elegantly finished a ship as has floated on the waters of Port Jackson is the ship *Neotsfield,* now here on her maiden voyage. As will be remembered from the previous notices, the *Neotsfield* is specially a Sydney ship, built to the order of Mr. Dangar, (Dangar, Gedy and Co.) for this trade, and registered in this port. It is not surprising, therefore, that more than an ordinary amount of interest is attached to the *Neotsfield*, and it is safe to say that all those who have seen her are highly pleased, and cannot speak in too loud terms of praise. Unquestionably when the ship comes to Circular Quay as she probably will today, she will attract the attention of a large number of shipping people.

As she brought up behind Garden Island yesterday she presented a remarkably fine appearance, her towering masts showing high above the high land of the island, as those who boarded her might have noticed when crossing the bay from Mrs. Macquarie's Chair. The first expression was that she looked very deep—"more like a Liverpool ship" full of heavy deadweight cargo than a London ship with lighter general merchandise. This is easily accounted for, as one item alone in her present immense cargo of close on 4,000 tons weight and measurement consists of 600 tons of pig iron. Still, deep as she undoubtedly is, she managed to log 310 knots with a whole sail breeze, and, as those on board remarked "What she would have done if flying along with a wool cargo, for instance, can only be conjectured".

Neotsfield's hull is iron, not steel, it being thought by her owners that greater strength is thus secured. As to strength she may be said to be the personification of it, being built under special survey, and at one of the first yards on the Clyde. No money has been spared in her construction, or in any part of her. A gracefully overhanging bow is terminated in a "horn" jibboom, underneath which is a prettily decorated curled figurehead, forming altogether one of the most pleasing looking bows possible to imagine. The entrance is moderately fine and the run particularly so, indeed some considerable sacrifice of carrying capacity was made to insure that this representative on the ocean hailing from Sydney, New South Wales should show clean heels to anything on the road. The ship sits well in the water and shows her well-formed sheer to advantage. Once on deck one is struck by the fine clear space there is on board, stretching away forward to the break of the topgallant forecastle from the break of the poop aft. The splendid beam and great length are seen to advantage. Of the masts and spars it may be said that all the lower masts are steel, also the topmasts and lower yards of the fore and main masts; but not so the mizzen, the topmast and topgallant mast, which are of wood. Not a day is to be lost by Messrs. Dangar, Gedy & Co., in sending her away to London. A large part of her wool is in store, and she will begin to land her inward cargo today, and loading operations will speedily follow.

RODNEY

THE two dominating personalities of the nineteenth century great shipbuilding yards of Sunderland, were James Laing and William Pile, both born in the same year, 1823. Both men came from shipbuilding families. William Pile as a boy occupied most of his time making ship models. In 1848, he commenced building on his own account ships of wood. In 1860, he converted his yard for the introduction of iron, launching his first iron ship in 1861. His business became tremendous and was the largest on the Wear River being equipped with eight building slips employing 2,000 men and boys.

Pile built many famous ships for the tea and wool trades where speed was so essential. Their beauty of design and appearance made them remembered as the perfection of the shipbuilders' art. His two best known were the composite-built *Torrens* for the Adelaide trade in 1868, and the iron *Rodney* for the Sydney trade in 1874.

Joseph Conrad joined the *Torrens* as second mate in 1891, and wrote of her:—

> "The way the ship had of letting big seas slip under her did one's heart good to watch. It resembled so much an exhibition of intelligent grace and unerring skill that it could fascinate even the least seamanlike of our passengers".

Pile's masterpiece, *Rodney* was built to the order of Devitt and Moore, who later claimed her to be the fastest ship in their fleet. Her passenger accommodation was well ahead of her time. The cabins were carpeted and even bedding was provided. The first class area extended 80 feet under the poop deck. The second and

Ship *Rodney*, minus figurehead, lost in bad weater off the Horn.

third class were in the 'tween decks below. Tables and seats in the saloon were removable for dancing; a piano provided the music. There was even a large bathroom for hot baths; a welcome innovation of the day was a steam condenser distilling 500 gallons of fresh water daily. With a large complement of live stock comprising chickens, ducks, geese, pigs and a milking cow; little wonder that *Rodney* was a favourite passenger ship. Pity the cow, however, the heaving decks of a ship would be a poor substitute for a green field of England. It has been recorded from a vessel on a voyage surrounded by heavy fog and icebergs, that the foghorn was continually sounded, but to the consternation of the captain and his officers, the echo came back from dead ahead no matter whether the helm was to starboard or port. It was discovered that the "echo" was from the cow penned on the fore end of the ship. No doubt the sound of the foghorn brought back fond memories for the lonely cow.

Rodney had her share of tempestuous weather with passengers battened down below with heavy seas sweeping over her decks. On her last voyage she lost her figurehead, an effigy of a lion

In 1889 she made a name for herself by passing *Cutty Sark*.

A bow view of *Rodney*, in dry dock. A fine illustration of iron ship building, with overlapping plates
and flush rivetting.

Rodney, appears about to receive a mountainous sea on the port quarter near Cape Horn, on her last passage from Australia in 1886, when she was badly knocked about by the high seas.

Sailors on the main yard bending a mainsail to the jackstay. On a foot rope of a swaying spar, it was a case of one hand for the ship and the other for yourself, but more often two hands for the ship.

The two clippers alternately gained the advantage, *Rodney* finally arriving at Gravesend one hour behind *Cutty Sark*.

Under such conditions it is difficult to assess the speed of a ship, one compared to another. Wind variations of two miles can make a difference as experienced by the tea clippers of the famous 1866 race. *Taeping* and *Fiery Cross* were becalmed in the doldrums. *Fiery Cross* watched *Taeping* pick up a breeze and sail out of sight in a few hours. For *Fiery Cross* there was no movement except a bluish haze emanating from the poop deck caused by seamanlike rhetoric from a frustrated Captain Robinson watching *Taeping* sail away.

In the *Rodney*, sailing in fine weather meant many happy days for the passengers on deck. They were entertained by officers and apprentices in various sports and life on board would have provided happy memories to last a lifetime. The splendid photographic series of deck scenes speak for themselves, placing

The mate of *Rodney*, steadies himself against the rail during heavy weather off Cape Horn. A canvas shelter is lashed in the mizzen rigging for his protection. No sails on foremast, no head sails.

Captain Corner of the *Rodney*, prepared for heavy weather on deck. He was a fine example of a first class seaman and sailing ship master. "my mother **told** me not to go to sea!"

H

on record what life was like on a crack clipper ship. On this her last voyage under the Devitt and Moore flag, *Rodney* encountered the worst weather of her career. Mountainous seas crashed aboard, bulwarks were carried away under the weight of water, live stock pens were washed overboard and the decks became a mass of wreckage which was swept backwards and forwards to the danger of the seamen hauling on the gear.

Below, the tables, seats and the piano breaking adrift plus the idescribable noise of the seas pounding on the deck above, would no doubt have left an indelible mark on the passengers' memories even more so than the days and nights of serenely sailing along under tropical stars and skies.

At the completion of the 1896 voyage, when *Rodney* berthed in London Docks, the chief officer, Mr. Groves, called "That'll do men", which meant the end of voyaging under the Red Ensign.

Rodney was sold to French owners in 1897, and renamed *Gypsy*. On 7th December, 1901, she was wrecked on the rugged Cornish coast when homeward bound from Iquique with a nitrate cargo. All the crew was saved but *Gypsy*, ex-*Rodney* became a total loss.

A pair of albatrosses.

This poor old albatross, provided entertainment for some strung up by its beak, on the *Rodney*.

Passengers playing roulette on *Rodney*. The names of the passengers as numbered are: 1-Davies, 2.-Wildshaw, 3-Panet, 4-Bain, 5,-Hanley, 6-Main, 7- Miss Fielding, 8-Jeff. Miss Fielding's great grand-daughter in similar circumstances would no doubt be bikini clad and very much in the foreground.

Apprentices entertaining *Rodney* passengers, with an energetic potato race. The apprentice shows a good leg for the enjoyment of the ladies. Today, crew members, in reverse are entertained by the ladies. Our great grandfathers, were lucky if they saw so much as an ankle.

On the poop deck of *Rodney*. Apprentice Hughes and able seaman Denton are oiling the deck. Senior apprentice Roxby is at the wheel. Third Mate is against the rail with two passengers, Wildshaw and Jeff.

PORT JACKSON

ABOUT noon, on 6th May, 1770, at a distance of two or three miles, Captain Cook sighted an opening in the Australian coast line between two headlands which he correctly assumed to be a harbour and named it Port Jackson after the Deputy Secretary of the Admiralty. This was the first naming of the harbour which has become known as one of the greatest natural harbours of the world.

Over 100 years later in 1882, the name Port Jackson was bestowed on a splendid four mast barque at her launching. Designed by Alexander Duthie for the famous shipping firm of Duthie Brothers of Aberdeen so well known in the Australian trade at that time, she was built by Messrs, Hall and Co. also of Aberdeen, at a cost of £28,000, without any stinting. This was considered to be a high price for those days.

Of iron construction *Port Jackson* had a characteristic in the shape of the old style of rigging set up to chain plates and channels on the outside of the hull. This gave added strength to her masting and also made her easily identifiable. With such a name, the nautically minded people of Sydney maintained a personal interest into the career of the *Port Jackson* especially when she became a welcome and familiar sight in Sydney Harbour.

Port Jackson sailed on her maiden voyage to Sydney in 77 days from the English Channel. This was a record at that time for a four mast barque. Originally intended for the emigrant trade her 'tweendeck had a height of 8½ feet with full provision made for ventilation by the installation of portholes from one end of the ship to the other. *Port Jackson* could have accommodated 700

The Port Jackson, has dropped the tow rope and is on the starboard tack with the yards braced hard round against the port backstays.

passengers providing more comfortable quarters than was then usual. The fittings of the five 2-berth cabins were of birds-eye maple mahogany. Her spars were rigged to perfection and, except for a gale in the Bay of Biscay, carried her royals for the whole of her maiden voyage. She carried a long gibboom and in the fashion of the day, steeve downwards. To accentuate the fashion, the mate, on a later passage, tightened up the martingales underneath, to such an extent that he split the jibboom, followed by some mutterings from the ship's carpenter.

Port Jackson's voyages for the next few years were good ones without incidents until 1893, when moored alongside a wharf in Darling Harbour, Sydney, a fire broke out in her lower hold. When the after hatch was opened a thick pall of smoke poured out. Local firemen were sent below wearing repirators which were ineffective. The firemen, in an exhausted state were hauled out after four minutes. An attempt was then made to bore a hole in the deck but iron plating between the deck planking and the beams prevented access. (At least, the iron plating proved that *Port Jackson* was one of the strongest iron ships ever built). Five steam fire engines then pumped water down the hatches at the rate of 2,000 gallons per minute until the water level reached the coamings of the 'tween deck. Main deck plating and deck beams were warped by the heat, 100 feet of lower deck plating was burnt and there was considerable damge to the main deck planking. The cost of repairs was estimated at over £4,000 with £15,000 worth of cargo damage. Fortunate indeed, that a fire of this magnitude occurred alongside a wharf with effective fire fighting equipment available instead of in mid-ocean where the hazards of fire are dreaded.

Port Jackson was laid up by her owners for two years owing to steep competition by the tramp steamers. In 1904, she was purchased by Devitt and Moore for sail-training purposes and was fitted out to accommodate 100 boys whose ages ranged from 14 to 18 years. The commencement of the voyage was disastrous when she was cut almost to the water line by a colliding steamer. However, *Port Jackson* proved to be a fine training ship and many Masters and officers owed a great deal to their having trained under the flag of Devitt and Moore.

There followed a number of highly succesful voyages of a similar nature until she was sold out of the service in 1916, at the age of 34 years.

Sailing ships during the First World War were pressed into service! *Port Jackson* was sent to Buenos Aires and sailed from there on 17 January, 1918, with a cargo of wheat for the U.K. On 28th April she was sunk by a German submarine. The mate and 14 men were picked up, but the Captain and the remaining. 12 were never heard of again.

MOUNT STEWART

INSPIRED by the importance of the Australian wool industry the Golden Fleece Line of wool clippers owned by A. J. Carmichael, played a tremendous part in shipping wool to the London Markets. Between 1868 and 1886, they ordered thirteen iron clippers from the builders Barclay Curle & Co. of Glasgow. Among this group were the *Mermerus* and *Argonaut* both much admired for their good looks, as were all of Barclay Curle's creations. In 1891, these fine ship builders surpassed themselves by producing two sky sail yard ships, the *Mount Stewart* and *Cromdale*.

Of the later day wool carriers, the *Mount Stewart* was one of the best known and earned for herself a great deal of affection in the hearts of the shipping fraternity wherever she sailed. *Mount Stewart* and her sister ship *Cromdale* were the last two ships to be built for the Australian wool trade. Designed to carry large cargoes, they were of necessity not so fine lined as their predecessors but nevertheless were beautifully proportioned. Built of steel, perfectly sparred with a skysail yard at the main, they were a delight to any sailor's eye.

An apprentice on the *Mount Stewart* gave a valuable and interesting account of the life at sea in a letter to his father which was published in a Sydney newspaper. He gave a vivid account of a squall encountered when the ship was nearing Cape Horn:—

> "This Sunday the boys were keeping day look-outs and it was mine from two o'clock till four in the afternoon. The weather was nice and fine and I went up in pants, singlet and seaboots with my oilskins over my arm. It had just gone seven bells and I was

The *Mount Stewart*, famous wool carrier.

thinking that I would have a sleep in the dog watch, when the mate came forrard to pull on jibsheets. Mind you, there was a fair breeze blowing but he had only just got onto the forecastle head when it fell a dead calm. The "old man" had just gone up on to the poop and was looking up aloft. He walked to the wheel and as I heard afterwards, told the helmsman that he expected a bit of a blow. The ship was then under topsails and staysails. He next turned to the lee side and I happened to look the same way. On the horizon I could see nothing but one mass of froth and tremendous waves. The 'old man' turned. "Stand by topsail halyards lower the yards half down ", he shouted at the same time motioning the wheel hard over. In three seconds the storm had struck us. Talk about hail and spray storms, you could not beat it and we were nearly caught aback when it would have been time to say our prayers. The fore topsails blew away at once, making a noise like guns firing and I can tell you I didn't feel exactly at my ease. After the fore topsails had gone the 'old man' got the mizzen topsails in safe when the main upper blew away. The winds and the seas were something terrific. Every time she rolled, under went the lee rail taking huge dollops which swept the ship from rail to rail. I was shivering on the foc's'cle head; the weather was as cold as ice, absolutely freezing, and I had hail and spray dashing into my face all the time for seven and a half hours while all hands were aft on the poop. Something had gone wrong with the mizzen staysail sheet and two hands were sent on deck to attend to it. The first on deck a seaman named Reginald Ick, an Australian and a nice young fellow, jumped on to the spar at the weather main braces to see to it and in doing so got a weather sea on top of him and before he had time to get off the spar, the weather rail went under and a big sea sent him head first overboard. The other seamen yelled to the mate who flung a couple of lifebelts but of no avail. The mountainous seas prevented a boat from being launched and we had to lope ahead. The 'old man' did his best to put the ship around, but all hands could hardly move the yards. At midnight the wind died down gradually but the sea was still big—Then came a time of holystoning, tarring down, cleaning, chipping, scraping and painting; and every night in the second dog watch the 'old man' had the boys aft on the poop and taught them to box".

Such was the life at sea, an existence of extreme hardship for the older men who knew no other way of life but high adventure for the apprentices which was what they sought by going to sea.

Captain McColm and his ship survived the many dangers of the First World War.

For as long as it was possible to get a wool or grain cargo *Mount Stewart* was left in the Sydney-London trade and in 1923, was ordered to Liverpool where many an old salt was delighted to see her again (especially as she was one of the last half dozen deep water sailing ships still flying the Red Ensign). One more passage to Sydney and finally she was sold to shipbreakers at Nantes. This was a real heartbreak for many of the old seamen who knew no other home.

Captain McColm retired with his wife and two young sons to a dairy farm in New South Wales.

In 1924, a good looking young man seeking adventure on the high seas signed on the articles as a cadet for a voyage around the world in the *Mount Stewart*. He was known to his shipmates as Charlie Howard. His full name was Charles, Henry, George Howard, Earl of Suffolk and 14th Earl of Berkshire. During the Second World War, Charlie Howard demonstrated courage and sacrifice of the highest order. He was killed defusing a bomb for which he was awarded the George Cross posthumously.

MARCO POLO

"*M*ARCO *Polo*, —The largest vessel ever despatched from Liverpool to Australia: and expected to sail as fast as any ship afloat", was the announcement in the first Shipping Notice of this truly remarkable ship, later regarded as the maritime wonder of the day.

She was built by James Smith of St. John, New Brunswick, in 1851, as just another cargo ship but Smith did depart from the usual design in that he gave her a sharper underwater body. She was even regarded by her builders as a very ordinary wooden ship. After her frames were erected and ready for planking a violent gale blew them down and they had to be set up again. More trials and tribulations followed for the foreman shipwright when at her launch in April 1851, she got out of control and ran up on the opposite bank of the creek, heeled over on her beam ends, causing injury to some people on board. She was eventually hauled off and found to be slightly hogged. With her heavy bricklike above waterline hull form, everybody concerned was inclined to disown such an unpromising and so unsightly a ship, but, after she had made her reputation as a Black Ball liner, those who formerly denied interest in her were just as vociferous in claiming credit for her speediness.

The St. John Shipping register records on 26th May, 1851: *Marco Polo* 1625 tons. Three decks and a half poop. Length 184·1 ft. Breadth amidships 36·3. Depth of hold amidships 29·4 ft. Standing bowsprit. Square sterned without galleries. When she left St. John her bows were adorned with a full length figure of the Venetian explorer, Marco Polo. There were no other decorations, but when she became a Black Ball liner some carvings were placed upon her stern; an elephant's head in the centre flanked by reclining figures of Marco Polo himself.

Marco Polo made her maiden voyage to Liverpool. She recrossed the Atlantic for a cargo of cotton and after the return passage to Liverpool she was eventually bought by the young and enterprising James Baines who had her completely fitted out as an emigrant ship. Her dining saloon was fitted out in the height of opulence with maple ceilings and richly ornamented pilasters. There was a profusion of stained glass panels in the saloon and a plate glass table in the centre allowed light to penetrate to the dormitories below—nothing but the best for James Baines' line of ships. He was fortunate to obtain a charter for the whole of the accommodation to the Government Emigration Commissioners, which meant a passenger list of 930 selected emigrants.

James Baines had great faith and enthusiasm in his project and went to great pains to provide ventilation to the emigrants' quarters as well as a sick bay with two qualified surgeons; consideration and comfort indeed for those days. He further proved his good judgment when he selected Captain John Nicol Forbes as Master. 'Bully' Forbes, as he came to be known in the Australian trade, was a superb seaman of exceptional ability. A strong and domineering character who also gained notoriety later in his career. However, Captain Forbes and his ship proved to be one of those combinations that created maritime history. Some credit must go to the designer of the ship, but it seems that her success was really due to the driving ability of her master.

Marco Polo left Liverpool on 4th July, 1852, the largest ship to sail to Australia. Before sailing, the usual banquet was held on board and in a speech, Forbes predicted that *Marco Polo* would be in the Mersey again within six months. This was more **important** than the record passage to Melbourne of 68 days. The fact that a ship had made the round voyage in less than six months was of vital significance. Those were the goldrush days, when people of the Old World wanted a quick passage to Melbourne, and with shipping so much in demand quick passages were the order of the day. When *Marco Polo* was hauled into the dock at Liverpool on completion of the round voyage the quays were crowded with people amidst an atmosphere of great excitement. Between her foremast and mainmast a huge strip of canvas was suspended with the inscription painted in huge letters—"The fastest ship in the World".

The *Marco Polo* brought home £100,000 in gold dust. Her reputation was made and visitors came from far and wide to visit this marvel of the sea. Her advertisements for the second voyage now had her promoted to the status of "the celebrated clipper ship, *Marco Polo*", a far cry from the nondescript vessel launched from the unglamourous March Creek of St. John, New Brunswick.

Her second voyage was another good one with 648 passengers and £90,000 of specie. She left Melbourne again with £280,000 of gold dust and again achieved a time of six months for the round voyage. Bully Forbes again received a vociferous welcome from the merchants. At this stage Bully Forbes was promoted to command of the new *Lightning* and was succeeded by his chief mate, McDonnell, who also made a good round voyage. Her succeeding masters were not sail carriers of the calibre of Forbes and McDonnell; the ship was becoming badly strained and could not stand up to the hard driving.

In 1861, *Marco Polo* collided with an iceberg and was severely damaged almost to the point of abandonment. Her bowsprit had carried away, the bow was stove in and the foremast sprung. She managed to struggle into Valparaiso after a month's constant pumping. After repairs she arrived in Liverpool in 183 days out.

There was life in the old ship yet, for in 1867, she made a fine passage from Australia beating the *Great Britain* by eight days. She had made the passage in 76 days, *Marco Polo* finished her days in the Canadian lumber trade with chains fastened around the hull to help keep her together.

There were many hazards for the sailor in his rough and tumble life at sea and the 2nd mate of *Marco Polo* bought some real trouble for himself when he decided to snare a shark that was following the ship. A baited hook was the means of hauling the shark alongside. A bowline was slipped over his body and hooking on to a tackle, the big fish was hauled over the rail on to the monkey poop. Then the action really began. The 16 ft. shark showed fight and stove in the cabin skylight with a fierce blow of his tail. The sailors on deck were frantically endeavouring to curb the shark's activity when it suddenly vanished through the broken skylight into the cabin below. In rushed the carpenter who made a vigorous swing with his axe but missed, the blade cutting deeply into the cabin floor which was completely mutilated in the ensuing battle between Chips and the shark, with the apartment a complete wreck, the floors and walls stained with blood and slime, the table smashed, cabin panelling stove in, the shark was at last dragged out on to the main deck, and the 2nd mate subjected to a typical flow of "Blue Nose" language from the deeply incensed Captain, aroused from his sleep by the commotion.

On 22nd July 1883, spectators on shore at Prince Edward Island, in the Gulf of St. Lawrence were astounded to see a large ship with all sails set heading for the shore, as soon as she grounded her crew cut away the rigging and away went the masts and yards to leeward. Boats put off from the shore and the crew were brought in.

They gave as their reason for grounding, that they were in fear of the ship which was leaking badly, and would founder as the pumps had broken down. So ended, ignominiously, the career of *Marco Polo* built as a timber ship that had in her prime, earned for herself the reputation of being the fastest ship in the world.

LA HOGUE

IN the all-important immigrant trade to Australia, the *La Hogue* transported many thousands of new settlers from the old world to the new. Each year she was a familiar sight at Circular Quay. Always a comfortable and well-found ship, she was greatly favoured and was ideal as a passenger ship. She was built by Laing of Sunderland for the great Duncan Dunbar, who in 1855, owned a fleet of sailing ships totalling 40,000 tons, of which only a few exceeded 1,000 tons—a tremendous fleet for those days.

La Hogue's characteristics included a 96 foot poop believed to be the largest of any sailing ship at that time and ideal for the promenading passengers. Her immense figurehead was the yellow lion-rampant of Dunbar's house-flag, supporting a shield emblazoned with the St. Andrew's cross. Her larger than usual timber frames of English oak and India teak were strengthened by iron bars running from gunwale to keel on the outside at 30 degrees and at opposite angles on the inside. This idea seemed to be a forerunner of the composite designed ship soon to follow (wood planking on iron frames). Over twenty tons of copper were used on the bottom with sixty tons of iron knees for supporting the timbers.

The launching was an event of great enthusiasm as demonstrated by this newspaper report—written in the quaint mid-Victorian style of the day:—

"The music from an instrumental band gave exquisite pleasure. Shortly afterwards was heard the familiar rattle of the carpenter's hammers which announced that the last shore was about to be driven out. In a minute the rope at bow was cut, the

114

iron blocks fell down, out flew the remaining shore and in a moment the towering fabric took the water 'as a bird that seeketh its mother's nest', greeted by cheers from the yard and from hundreds of spectators who lined the opposite bank of the river".

Her voyaging of thirty years was to Port Jackson, except on one occasion when she took 500 passengers to Wellington, N.Z. in 1874.

Her first commander was Captain Williams who was responsible for her reputation as a happy ship. Consequently, passengers were prepared to wait months for a berth in her in preference to another ship. Captain Williams eventually retired after a distinguished career as a very able commander and was succeeded by his first officer, Mr. Goddard.

At the time of her launching in 1855, *La Hogue* was not only the largest ship built at Sunderland but she was the most advanced in shipbuilding technique. Sunderland on the river Wear in England, has a remarkable shipbuilding history. The year

La Hogue, a popular passenger ship which features in many family records.

1346, was a year of victories for England. King Edward III, had defeated the French army at Crecy and six years before, the English had had a brilliant sea victory at Sluys. Edward, greatly encouraged by his victories on land and sea, demanded ships and more ships. This was the opportunity for one, Thomas Melvill, who occupied a place in Hendon, Sunderland, for the building of ships for which he paid the Bishop of Hatfield, an annual rent of two shillings. Thomas Melvill prospered and from that humble beginning grew the great shipbuilding industries of Sunderland.

Newspaper reports of the day enthused about *La Hogue*'s luxurious saloon, the airiness of the state rooms, her splendid system of ventilation and that every cabin was lighted with an oil lamp. Splendour indeed, for those days!

During her long life *La Hogue*'s passages, as regular as ferry boats, were remarkably free from accident. She was a worthy representative of the frigate-built hardwood East India passenger ship. Her poop was 96 feet long extending from the stern almost to the mainmast, an ideal romantic setting for dancing under the stars of a tropical evening, with lanterns lashed to the rigging providing just the right atmosphere aided by the ship's band. Those were the days and evenings of delight lessening the anxieties of the immigrants for the uncertainties of the new life ahead.

La Hogue's last voyage as an immigrant ship was from Sydney, in 1888. Her sailing date was delayed for several weeks because of the Russian war scare. Captain Wagstaff with commendable thinking installed a cannon on board; no enemy was to be allowed to capture his ship. On board was a consignment of about 1,200 birds which poured forth a cacophony of screeching which came to an end when they were swept overboard in a gale off Cape Horn.

At the end of the voyage, *La Hogue* was sold to Madeira, as a coal hulk in 1897.

La Hogue is believed to have had the dubious distinction of transporting the first two rabbits to Australia, by some misguided passenger. Unfortunately, they were not washed overboard as was so much live stock from the clippers.

PARRAMATTA

THERE were many ships of the sailing ship era who seemed to acquire a distinct personality. Spoken of with admiration and affection, they received their crowds of visitors on Sundays and generally became great favourites in the Australian ports to which they traded. Such a ship was the *Parramatta*, the first ship built for the Devitt and Moore line in 1866. Built at Sunderland, *Parramatta*'s length overall was 231 ft. beam 38 ft. depth 23¾ ft., registered tonnage 1521.

Parramatta's first voyage was reported in the "Sydney Mail" as follows:—

FIRST ARRIVAL, DEC. 14, 1866

Captain Williams may be justly proud of this splendid ship which arrived on the 14th, after a most favourable passage considering the adverse weather she has experienced. She is without comparison the finest vessel that has ever reached this port, the strength and care with which she has been constructed being most remarkable and special attention has been directed to the passengers' accommodation which is perfect in every respect. Capt. Williams brings a full complement of First Class passengers together with a large and valuable cargo.

She was a first class Blackwall frigate-type of passenger ship which traded between London and Sydney year after year with the regularity of a ferry boat. She had a heavy stern with large cabin windows. The ship's topsides were painted black, with black ports on a white band, Navy fashion, white rail and deck

Parramatta, which carried many families to Australia.

fittings, bowsprit and lower masts. Even the boats were painted man-o'-war fashion with white bottoms and black topsides. Like most ships of her type, *Parramatta* had little or no sheer and the lower dead eyes of her rigging bolted through wide channels to chain plates which reached down almost to the water line. She had a long quarter deck which extended almost to the fife rail of the mainmast, a deck house on the same level and a long fo'c'sle deck which reached well aft. There was ample deck space—for working ship and for deck chairs for the passengers when they tired of promenading. There was also plenty of room of course for dancing.

Although *Parramatta* had the usual tremendous spar plan with stuns'ls, she was never driven to the extreme, as the first consideration of the Captain and the Devitt and Moore Line was for the comfort of the passengers. Consequently, *Parramatta* was always a happy comfortable ship, both for passengers and crew, and accommodation was always in demand, especially for families. Her passages were always consistently good, often well within eighty days. Her clean, coppered bottom no doubt contributed in no small measure to these excellent passages. During the early part of her career, *Parramatta* left Sydney for Cape Horn, but later on, adopted the more comfortable route around the Cape of Good Hope. In 1879, during the passage round Cape Horn, she was obliged to thread her way through a field of icebergs. In a sudden squall, she lost thirteen of her sails which were blown out of their bolt ropes creating pandemonium aloft with a tangle of gear. One unfortunate passenger lost all his washing to leeward.

Life on board ship was usually pleasant and interesting for the passengers. On the 1879 voyage to Sydney, they even produced a magazine "The *Parramatta* Serio-Comic Sun", conducted by George Arthur Musgrave. (The journal was later printed ashore in Sydney). The skeleton diary gives a splendid insight into the activities of the voyage.

From the journal:—
> SAT. SEPT. 20TH 1879
> Becalmed—sea dead smooth; Captain Goddard and Mr. Shardlow (1st Mate) with "Chips" off in a boat on a voyage of inspection around the ship. Very hot. At dinner Dr. Oakes after a preliminary flourish read the first number of the "The *Parramatta* Serio-Comic Sun". Sunset a magnificent study in reds, not a breath of air stirring, voices of crew marvellously distinct. A scratch concert going on after dark on the main deck. Concertina and bones.

Then by way of contrast:—
> FRI. OCT. 3RD
> 3 a.m. Sharp rain storm awoke all who had been asleep. In the black darkness scarred at intervals with angry lightning flashes and amidst a pandemonium of sounds. Roaring Captain—yelling officers—vocal crew—Multitudinous treading of feet—howling wind bumping of rollers—a wild scramble to make secure portholes. 6 a.m. A sky of wet clouds—inky surly sea. Ship tearing away W.—Officers wet and tired. Sun does not appear . . .

There were compensations for the ladies in finer weather. As viewed from their deckchairs, the cynosure of the ladies' eyes were the magnificent legs of seaman Jenkins as he walked by! (By contrast, our great grand-dads were lucky to even see a lady's ankle!) Today, the liberated ladies have "turned the tables".

> SEPT. 17TH, 1879
> Our good ship in throes all night, bulkheads creaking and groaning, doors slamming, wind howling, crew stamping overhead. Cabin floor strewed with books, clothes, music, boots, hats, etc, which had been adrift during night. On deck in morning, sight magnificent. Ship careering up and down the cobalt hills . . .

The final entry:—

DEC. 8TH

At 4.30 a.m. Mr. Shardlow's merry voice calls all on deck, and long before 6—almost everybody is on deck looking at the long range of cliffs through which is pierced the opening into Sydney Harbour. The sun rose in glory and a finer day was never seen on earth—everybody gay—excited—the Captain at length happy—the pilot chatty—and the little tug pulling away at us vigorously—our sails are all furled—manifestly our voyage is over—at 6 o'clock we pass from the open ocean between the heads of Sydney Harbour and at once experience that burst of beauty that has no equal in the world. The scene is new to many and for a time the loveliness of the surroundings takes away the now prominent feeling of sadness—the crepitant noise of the cicadas (or so called locusts)—the curious vegetation—the labyrinth of pretty little coves—the bright glitter of not far distant Sydney conspire to absorb the stranger. Soon we have boats alongside—friends long asunder are joined—a hurrying bustling exciting parting takes place—and before we can realise it, we have left the open sea, we are dispersing— Farewell coo-e-e-s and waving handkerchiefs greet us as we fall away from the noble ship in which we have gone through so many experiences.

To one and all, in closing this little fragmentary record of our pleasant association, we must heartily wish God speed.

In 1888, *Parramatta*, was sold to Norway and became a timber carrier, disappearing from the register in 1899, just after her famous commander, Captain Goddard, died in Sydney. Captain Goddard spent 14 years on the ship from 1874, and was extremely popular and capable.

PARRAMATTA'S COMPLEMENT

Officers and crew	67
Passengers—1st class	40
Nurses	2
Passengers—2nd class	51
Tweedy	1
Stowaway	1
TOTAL	162

It would be interesting to know what was a "Tweedy"? (One rank above that of a stowaway?)

SOBRAON

IN 1866, a clipper-ship was launched from the yard of Alexander Hall of Aberdeen. When fitted out, she sailed into the annals of maritime history as one of the great sailing ships of a remarkable era. Her name was *Sobraon*, a title which commemorated the decisive victory which ended the first Sikh war in 1845.

After the loss of the *Schomberg* which was the largest wooden ship ever built in England, Halls had not received an order for a large composite clipper for eleven years. This new one was very strongly built. The wire backstays on the *Sobraon* were galvanised and the chain plates were a double bar. Her registered tonnage was 2,131 tons; overall length 317 feet; length between perpendiculars 272 feet; beam 40 feet; depth of hold 27 feet. *Sobraon* was the largest composite ship built in England, and was a wonderful success for the whole of her sailing career to 1891. She was then sold to the N.S.W. government for £12,500 and converted to a reformatory ship and moored off Cockatoo Island. An average of 400 boys were trained on her at a time. The Commonwealth of Australia Government then bought her and renamed her H.M.A.S. *Tingira* (aboriginal for "open sea"). At a cost of £7,000 she was converted at Mort's Dock for a training ship for boys entering the Royal Navy. Some three thousand boys received their preliminary training on this ship which was a familiar sight at Rose Bay, Sydney for another sixteen years. She was sold in 1927, to Ford the boat-builder at Berry's Bay, where she lay until broken up in 1941. Unlike many of her contemporaries, she was never dismasted. A fine entrance and a beautiful run aft gave her excellent sailing qualities. She had been intended to be an auxiliary but that idea was eliminated by her

The *Sabraon*, at the time of her launch in 1886. Note the fidded royal mast and the Colling & Pinkney reefing gear on main top gallant.

designers and the aperture for the screw was filled in, this resulted in an even longer run aft. Had she been driven by a "Bully Forbes" type of master, she could easily have equalled the records of the big "Black Ballers". As it was, her master, Captain Elmslie was an extremely competent seaman and his main purpose, besides making good passages was to cater for the comfort of his passengers.

In 1867, *Sobraon* made a fast passage to Melbourne, reaching Cape Otway in 60 days. With a little more luck with the winds at that stage, she could have broken the record of the *Lightning*.

In 1889, when *Sobraon* was running her easting down in 45 degrees south, a terrific squall struck the ship and the wind shifted from the north-west to the south-west. The yards were trimmed but the wind blew the foresail clean out of the bolt ropes. To prevent following seas from overwhelming the ship, the

Captain ordered a storm foresail to be bent. Thirty seamen worked on the foreyard for four hours before the sail was bent and reefed.

During the night, a portion of the *Sobraon*'s port bulwarks was carried away, the main saloon skylight was smashed in, washing passengers below off their feet while they were striving to reach their cabins. A lifeboat 22 feet above the sea was washed away and a steel davit snapped off short. Such was the force of a heavy sea! The crew managed with the aid of life-lines, to prevent themselves being washed overboard.

The forward deckhouse was badly damaged; the storm lasted from Sunday to Wednesday. The passengers suffered, especially when the wind dropped and the sails could not prevent the ship's violent rolling in the mountainous seas.

Sobraon gained a reputation for being a speedy and comfortable ship for passengers. Her first five voyages were to Sydney, under charter to Devitt and Moore. In 1872, she was bought by them and diverted to the Melbourne run. Service in the company was much sought after by seamen. Their ships were well found and manned. The round voyages were regulated to once a year.

In 1867, when Captain Elmslie took command, *Sobraon*'s crew consisted of 4 mates, a surgeon, 8 apprentices, a carpenter, sailmaker, boatswain, 2 boatswain mates, donkey-man, chief steward, chief cook, butcher and butcher's mate, 12 cooks and stewards, two stewardesses, 26 able seamen, 4 ordinary seamen, and 2 boys.

James Cameron had been the foreman shipwright at her building and served on board for her 25 years of sea-going service.

The food was exceptionally good on the *Sobraon*. There was an ice-box containing 10 tons of ice, also a condenser for converting salt water to fresh.

For the benefit of the passengers there was a large stock population on board:—3 milking cows, as well as bullocks, sheep, pigs, geese, fowls, all of which meant a delectable dinner-table menu. The passengers participated in deck games and even cricket was played on her spacious decks. The social life on board

The *Sabraon*, in Cockatoo Dock Sydney, in 1891, at the completion of a long and successful career. She was the largest composite clipper ever built and was launched at Aberdeen in 1866.

An historic photograph! The last of the *Sobraon*, at Berry's Bay Sydney in 1941.

seemed to be a long round of gaiety, weather permitting. Magazines were published and they gave excellent pen-pictures of life on board a happy ship. Many interesting photographs were taken by Dr. Doyle, the ship's surgeon. These photographs alone provide an authentic record of a ship under sail plus the activities of her passengers.

Under Dr. Doyle's care, passengers and crew alike, were in good hands concerning sickness and accident, but, a medicine chest on display at the Maritime Museum at Gothenburg, Sweden, illustrates how a ship Captain of earlier days had to cope, when confronted with a health problem. He was required to look up the symptoms of a patient's illness and prescribe from a numbered bottle as called for. A somewhat sad case arose when the ship's carpenter was suffering from a malady requiring bottle number 15 which was, unfortunately, empty. Nothing daunted, the Captain made up a prescription from bottles 8 and 7 added together and was deeply troubled when he made port minus a good ship's carpenter.

(The first of a series of photographs of the *MacQuarie*).
Ship *MacQuarie*, under sail.

Seamen going aloft to furl sail, on *MacQuarie*.

Deck scene on *MacQuarie*, a passenger presenting a picture of sartorial splendour. Note the powerful rigging in the background.

Crew of *MacQuarie*, gather round to be photgraphed watching the ceremony of feeding the ship's cats.

Cadets on *MacQuarie*.

Deck scene on *MacQuarie*, at anchor in Neutral Bay, Sydney.

During her 27 years of voyaging there were only two fatal accidents which were the loss of two men in falls from aloft. Two other members of the crew also fell but survived. On one pitch black night a young woman slipped over the stern. The alarm was given and a boat was away from the ship in four minutes, but, with a swell running the search was futile. With the loss of only one passenger *Sobraon* had a remarkable record of safety.

Although capable of speedy passages that could equal other ships, the Captain preferred a more leisurely voyage for the comfort of his passengers. Pastimes for them were well organised. On her last voyage, a committee was formed with a time table for cricket, tennis, quoits and skittles on the deck, with music, draughts, cards and chess in the saloon. Dramatic and debating groups were formed; concerts, a bazaar and other entertainments were arranged.

Sobraon's voyages were so orderly and well-run that she was a favourite with the medical profession who often prescribed a voyage on her, for their patients' health. With the accent on entertainment so well conducted by the captain and his officers, *Sobraon*'s passages were in the nature of a cruise-ship of

A passenger
having his hair cut
on board the *MacQuarie*

A lively looking lot—cadets on *MacQuarie*.

latter-day popularity. In fact, a cruise-ship as such, goes back to 1884, when the *Tyburnia* was charted by the Pleasure Sailing Yacht Co. of England, for a trip to different parts of the world at a fee of a guinea a head per day. The *Tyburnia* later owned by Burns Philp & Co., finished her life as a hulk in Townsville, with some of her timbers finishing up as park seats on Magnetic Island. *Sobraon* was a magnificent example of ship-building and ship-management and all that was best.

The famous old clipper survived to the old age of 74 years. Had she been left alone as a hulk for another 2 or 3 decades, she would have been taken care of by loving hands and restored to her former glory as were the *Victory, Cutty Sark, Balclutha* and the *Constitution.* Tied up at her old berth at Circular Quay's south-west corner, she would have created a vision of splendour to delight the Sunday crowds around the Quay.

Fortuna, ex *MacQuarie,* in dry dock in Sydney in 1946. The person standing under the hull is the author, Cyril Hume. This ship was built at Blackwall, London, as the *Melbourne,* in 1875. She was an iron ship. Her name was changed to *MacQuarie,* in 1888 and under that name she carried a large number of cadets. In 1904, she was bought by a Norwegian firm and renamed *Fortuna,* and converted to barque rig. Finally she was used as a coal hulk in Sydney, from 1909 to 1953, when she was broken up.

The *Margaret Galbraith,* was built in Glasgow in 1868, for Shaw Savill & Co. and was mostly engaged in the New Zealand passenger trade. She was lost in 1905, enroute to Buenos Aires.

The famous immigrant ship *Lady Jocelyn*, loading at Port Chalmers. She carried troops to the Maori wars.

ANTIOPE

IN August 1866, a fine-lined iron sailing ship was launched from the yard of Reid, Glasgow, and was ceremoniously christened with the classic name of *Antiope*, which did not particularly please the superstitious old shellbacks of the day; her name was obviously interpreted by them to be "anti-hope", and how could she be anything but an unlucky ship?

However, this eventually proved to be an undeserved slander as *Antiope* continued her voyaging on a long and distinguished career gaining for herself a reputation as a speedy clipper ship and a prolific money earner. She was built to carry rice from Rangoon, as were the other ships of Messrs. Heaps' fleet of clipper ships.

Antiope was 242 ft. 3 in. in length, 38 ft. 4 ins. breadth, with a 23 ft. 7 ins. depth of hold. In dry dock, her beautiful fine entrance and graceful lines, with a sharp deadrise amidships showed that she had all the attributes of the fast sailing clippers of the '60's when speed was the predominating factor of ship design.

Her early voyages mainly comprised general cargo to Melbourne or Sydney, loading horses for Madrid, and then rice from Rangoon to the U.K.

During the '70's, *Antiope*'s passages were remarkably good, including one of 68 days from Liverpool to Melbourne which included ten days of frustration in the calms of the doldrums and her performances under Captain Withers for her first ten years were outstanding.

Antiope's passages under Captain Black were more leisurely, probably because he had his wife aboard. No doubt this had a restraining influence on him against the discomfort of reckless sail carrying. For that reason, some sailing ship owners disapproved of a Captain's wife sailing with him.

A view of *Antiope*, from astern.

Antiope, under sail with
a gentle breeze on her port quarter.

Captain Black's wife died at sea and to the Captain fell the appalling task of reading the burial service before the body was committed to the deep, while their children's attention was distracted elsewhere.

In 1883, with a change of ownership to Gracie Beazley and Co., her passages were varied to the ports of the world including San Francisco, where she picked up grain cargoes.

The time came in the late 1890's when the tramp steamers took over the trade and the *Antiope* was sold to a Captain Murray. Like all sailing clippers of the time, economies were forced upon her in the way of reduced canvas and stores, the ignominy of being reduced to barque rig and being made available for any sort of charter to anywhere.

Antiope was sold in 1904, to a syndicate in Victoria, British Columbia, and then traded around Pacific ports.

Although British owned, she was chartered by the Russian Government to carry a cargo to Vladivostock during the Russo-Japanese war.

As she was flying the Russian flag, she was promptly captured by the Japanese but later released, and was then commanded from 1905, by Captain Mathieson for the next ten years.

Captain Mathieson was a colourful personality and during the Second World War, was stationed in Sydney in command of the American supply ship *Weerooma*.

During his regime, *Antiope* nearly came to the end of her career when caught in severe gales which sent her on her beam ends. All hands, for their lives, were sent below to trim the coal to windward. The heavy seas cleared her decks, the midship house was stove in, boats were smashed, and the gear tangled in the wash ports. All sails were blown out of their gaskets and were in rags. By a mighty effort on the part of the crew, the ship was righted, the gear untangled and everything made shipshape again. The *Antiope* continued in the Pacific trade until 1915, when she was sold to the Paparoa Coal Co., of New Zealand.

Owing to the heavy shipping losses of the First World War, ship tonnage was very much in demand and she was then sold at a large profit to the Otago Rolling Mills. The 50 year old clipper was

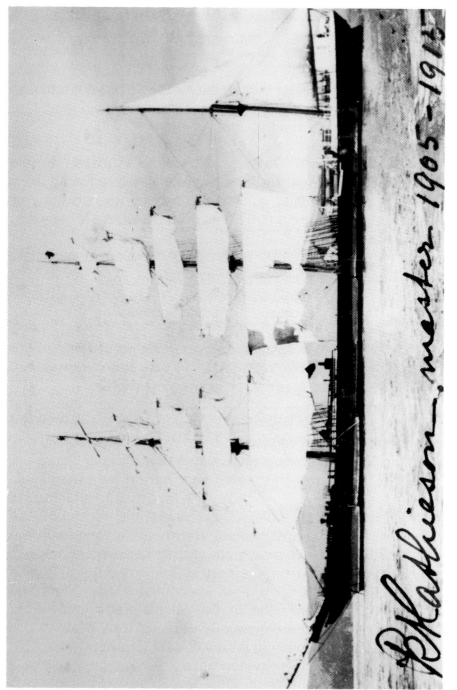

Antiope, showing sail damage, in San Francisco.

given a face lift and refit and went to Kaipara in North Auckland to load Kauri timber for Melbourne. From there she proceeded to Tasmania, with scrap iron and then took on a cargo of hardwood for the Bluff, in the far south of New Zealand. She signalled for a pilot on arrival there. However, the weather was too rough to take the pilot, but a tow rope was passed aboard. When the tug was only 100 yards from the Bluff wharf, a strong gust of wind blew the clipper on the rocks, and then the beach, where she lay on her side for three months. With soaring freights as an incentive, the owners decided to attempt a salvage operation.

The salvage engineers were called in, a steam and salvage barge was laid alongside, and everything was supposedly made tight over the hull damage. Pumping was commenced but without effect to the discouragement of the salvors, who stopped operations to consider what to do next, possibly with thoughts of abandoning the job.

But *Antiope*'s time was not yet. An inquisitive journalist named Bannerman, went below deck and as good luck would have it, the tide was at low ebb. In the darkness he could see a shaft of light coming through a hole in the hull. Amidst great excitement a mat was thrummed over the leak, the pumps were started and the ship slowly righted herself to the gratification of all concerned. After reconditioning, the old clipper took on a new lease of life, continuing her money-making voyages mostly between San Francisco and New Zealand.

A voyage to Rotterdam from Suva with copra and then a timber charter from the Baltic to Dalagoa Bay, Africa, was her last passage after fifty-five years of truly remarkable and wonderful service. *Antiope*, badly damaged by fire there, was finally fitted out as a store ship at Biera, there to end her days. So passed a famous clipper ship, who in her prime on one outward passage to Melbourne beat the times of the celebrated flyers *Thermopylae* and *Cutty Sark*.

The famous marine artist John Allcot, O.B.E., F.R.A.S., served in the *Antiope* and always maintained that she was the fastest of the clippers in her prime, which meant trouble for any listener who expressed doubt about that statement.

FANNY FISHER

IN 1845, John Nicholson, shipbuilder of the Upper Manning (Northern N.S.W.), signed a contract with Mr. Henry Fisher, Merchant of Sydney, to build a barque of 270 tons. This he did with all the skill and knowledge of his trade and to the best of his ability. At that time Nicholson's yard was at the riverside almost in the centre of Taree. Only a stone's throw away grew the giant black butts, ironbarks, blue gums and spotted gums which could be cut and fashioned in almost any way that the clever shipwright desired. Ti-tree for frames and crooks also grew close at hand and could be had for the launching of the giant barque. The vessel was to be 92 ft. long, 25 ft. beam, 14 ft. depth of hold and she was to be fashioned full and square like the old-time whalers.

The next two years were very busy ones for Mr. Nicholson and his shipwrights and sawyers. Mr. Fisher paid many visits to the yard to see his giant barge taking shape and loved to watch the chips and the sawdust fly, as the men, in their endeavours to do the best that could be done, pieced the hull together, frame by frame, strake by strake, beam by beam and plank by plank. They created a ship that had never been fashioned on the Manning River before, or the whole of the New South Wales coastline, for that matter. They were spurred on to do a good job for a good shipmaster because the success of their homeland depended on the seamen, the ships and the produce of the land, which even in those early days were sent 12,000 miles or more across the oceans.

There was another reason for haste. A rival ship-builder, Alexander Newton, was building a barque of similar lines and about the same dimensions downriver.

The foremen and master craftsmen from each yard would no doubt visit each other and stand off at vantage points where the lines of hulls could be seen and viewed with critical eyes. Each ship had a one piece keel and keelson, that had been cut from an ironbark tree with a straight barrel 130 feet long and six or more feet in diameter.

The day came when both were ready for launching and almost at the same time to the accompaniment of many cheers, they slid into the quiet waters of the Manning with flags and bunting flying in the breeze.

The *Fanny Fisher* was probably named after Mr. Fisher's daughter who, no doubt, was also represented by the shapely figurehead. The rival barque was named *Rosetta*.

Curiously the two barques finished their loading, took aboard their passengers and crossed the Manning bar on the same tide on the afternoon of September 8, 1847 and raced south to

The *Fanny Fisher*, 1845-1906. The photograph, appears to show her on one of the northern rivers of New South Wales.

Sydney. Captain Patrick of the *Rosetta* overran the Heads so Captain Harrold entered Port Jackson first.

. Three months then were spent on each barque outfitting them for inter-colonial trade, the *Fanny Fisher* loading for Wellington, and the *Rosetta* for Auckland. Each carried a full complement of passengers and they were considered commodious and beautiful vessels for those days.

The *Fanny Fisher*'s rig at that time would be single topsails, then changed to a patent reefing gear and later to double topsails.

One of *Fanny Fisher*'s masters was a colourful character named Frank Lopez who wore gold earrings. Captain Lopez, a Portuguese, took great pride in his ship and called her *Fanna da Fish*. He was over six feet tall and exceptionally strong. As a young man he was washed overboard in the English Channel and was picked up next day by another ship. Years later he survived the wreck of the *Harriet Armytage* on the oyster bank at Newcastle. Lopez dived overboard, battled through the heavy seas and swam into Newcastle. A third time, he narrowly escaped drowning when a small coaster foundered off Bondi and he swam two miles to the shore.

Fanny Fisher had a long and varied career, serving her owners well and profitably over 60 years. She was engaged in carrying good quality coal to the gas works in Darling Harbour, for many years. In the early '70s she was engaged on whaling cruises around Norfolk Island for eleven months at a time securing 70 tons of oil on one successful voyage.

On another whaling voyage in 1874, she was caught in a violent gale off Norfolk Island and lost two boats, plus the greater portion of the whale alongside.

Fanny Fisher was so seaworthy and reliable that her insurance rates were lower than other ships.

The day came in 1907, when shipbreakers took over John Nicholson's masterpiece and she was broken up at Folly Point, Middle Harbour, Sydney.

The name *Fanny Fisher* will always be remembered in the annals of Australian maritime history, for she was a fine example of a Colonial built ship from Australia's great days of sail.

ROYAL TAR

O N the beautiful river at Nambucca, North Coast of N.S.W., in 1876, a group of people, with mixed feelings and pride, watched a well-built and graceful ship slide down the launching ways and into the water. With her sleek black topsides, clipper bow, frames and timbers of blue gum and bloodwood, copper fastened, with yellow metal sheathing on her underbody, she was a beautiful sight. Named *Royal Tar*, she was to take her place in the panorama of Australian history as did many of her sisters built along the coast line of N.S.W.

Royal Tar was 598 registered tonnage, 171·2 ft. length, 31·4 ft. breadth and 17·2 ft. depth and was considered to be one of the largest wooden ships built in N.S.W. Her builder was a Mr. John Campbell Stuart, a skilful and capable master of his trade who had emigrated from Nova Scotia. *Royal Tar* was built to the order of Mr. W. Marshall, Engineer, and curiously, the Lloyds Register of Shipping, places both builder and owner in the wrong order, as indignantly asserted by Stuart's descendents.

The new ship's first venture to the open sea was not without difficulty as the depth of water on the bar was only seven feet. Barrels and tanks were lashed to the hull to float her higher and give clearance to her keel over the sandbar. The little coaster *Alchemist* took *Royal Tar* in tow but unfortunately the tow rope parted through entanglement with the screw of the steamer. *Royal Tar* finished up on the beach but finally was hauled off ten days later and towed to Sydney by the steamer, *Agnes Irving*. There, damage incurred to the hull was repaired.

Her maiden voyage was from Sydney to Newcastle where her arrival was June 13, 1878, and she was described as a schooner, also that her spars were salvaged from the schooner, *S.M.*

The *Royal Tar*, under sail off Auckland, New Zealand.

Stetson, previoulsy wrecked on Lord Howe Island. Apparently, in a short space of time, she was refitted as a barque with yards on fore and mainmast, which rig she carried throughout her career.

Her early years of voyaging were regular and money making for her owner, her cargoes being mostly timber. All was well until 1890, when she was chartered to take coal to New Guinea and then proceed in ballast to San Francisco to bring back a cargo of lumber. After discharging her cargo, Captain Franklin and the mate, Rodgers with members of the crew, decided to go shooting in the bush against all advice. The *Royal Tar* had hardly put to sea when the Captain and the mate, with most of the crew went down with a virulent type of malaria fever. Franklin and Rodgers died within a few days with the remainder of the crew being so sick that Nicholl, the second mate and two sailors were left to work the ship to San Francisco. After a long and protracted voyage, at times drifting helplessly, the *Royal Tar* reached port. They then encountered severe quarantine precautions even to the point where the authorities wanted to sink the ship! Adverse

Royal Tar, in Adelaide, prior to her second voyage to Paraguay, South America, in 1893.

publicity brought about a situation of some months of enquiries between San Francisco authorities, the Marine Board of Sydney and Mr. James Booth, her managing owner, the latter being completely exonerated from charges of not having provided sufficiently for a long voyage. The *Royal Tar* was sailed back to Sydney with her lumber in command of the newly promoted Captain John Nicholl.

The 1893, *Royal Tar* participated in the great adventure of William Lane and his band of socialists who were dissatisfied with living conditions in Australia and decided to sail for a new Australia in far-away Paraguay. This fascinating facet of Australian history is completely recorded by Mr. Gavin Souter in his excellent book, "A Peculiar People". *Royal Tar* carried out her part with efficiency and distinction. She made two voyages laden down with deck cargo and emigrants, one passage from Sydney and the other from Adelaide around the treacherous and dangerous waters of Cape Horn.

Upon her return, *Royal Tar* changed ownership and sailed under the flag of J. J. Craig of Auckland and was employed trading between New Zealand and Australia. On the early morning of November 26, 1901, when sailing from Auckland to Kaipara in ballast, the *Royal Tar* struck the submerged Shearer Rock, about 41 miles north of Tiritiri Island near Auckland.

Rockets were sent up and two lifeboats and a dinghy were launched and boarded by Mrs. Morrison and infant son, along with the crew. Captain Morrison remained on board with the mate. The holds were filled with water within twenty minutes. The mate, Rushly, decided to go below to retrieve his personal belongings before the cabin was filled. While he was below, the barque slipped off the rock into deep water taking the mate with her. Captain Morrison dived overboard and was picked up by one of the boats. The mishap was attributed to a fast running tide, as the course had been set at midnight to clear the rock. So passed a beautiful example of Australian pioneer shipbuilding.

She went down with all square sails set, into the darkness of Davy Jones' Locker and apparently into oblivion; or so it seemed, because now, through the enterprise of two young New Zealanders, Wade Doak and Kelvin Tarlton, portions of the *Royal Tar* have now been recovered by diving, after 68 years. On the first dive, an 18 lb. carronade was brought to the surface but this was probably carried either as ballast or for signalling. The two enterprising young men have now set up a museum in the Bay of Islands, a replica, one hundred feet long, in the form of the *Royal Tar* herself, to perpetuate the memory of the little barque.

Emigrants and friends about three days before departure of *Royal Tar*, for South America.

THE CLIPPER BRIG *WAVERLEY*

ALL seamen of the sailing era loved the brigs. With fore and mainmast only and a huge spread of canvas that dwarfed the shapely hull, their general appearance was a delight to a seaman's eye and they were always an object of admiration and affection.

The clipper brig *Waverley*, owned and registered in the Port of Sydney, was held in this high esteem and she was the aristocrat of the innumerable small craft that traded from port to port around the Australian coast line from the '60s to the '80s of the last century.

The brig has always been regarded as an efficient and manoeuvrable rig for deep sea sailing and for that reason was very much associated with the romance and adventure of the South Seas, from missionary work to the nefarious dealings of the South Sea pirates such as Captain Bully Hayes and Captain Ben Pease. Bully Hayes owned and commanded the smart little brig *Leonora* which figured on many of his shady exploits.

The owner of the *Waverley* was the colourful Captain Louis T. Castle, a well known resident of the suburb of Waverley who lived with his family in Bon Accord Avenue. A family story relates how Captain Castle and his attractive wife were walking down Pitt Street when who should loom up in front of them but Bully Hayes himself, who was not backward in casting a lascivious eye over Mrs. Castle. The incensed Captain Louis shaped up to Captain Bully, but friends prevented what could have been the best 'blue' in Pitt Street for many a year.

Captain Castle was very proud of his clipper brig, declaring her to be the most perfectly built and fitted out ship he had ever sailed on.

Built by Duncan of Garmouth, Scotland, of all wood construction, *Waverley* had a beautiful sheer accentuated by the top strakes, at the waterline, of the yellow metal sheathing which covered the whole of the under water body as a protection against marine growth and the destructive ravages of the sea worm. Her measurements were as follows: Registered tonnage 216, length 111 ft., beam 23·8 ft. and 13·8 ft. depth of hold.

In her earlier days *Waverley* traded to China ports, and as was customary, carried an armoury of boarding pikes, cutlasses and muskets and also two highly polished brass cannons for the purpose of discouraging piratical junks. The only time that cannons were put to use, except as signal guns, was on a voyage between Java and Australia.

The *Waverley* was caught in foul weather and a succession of water spouts bore down on her. The cannons were brought to bear and on discharge, the water spouts co-incidentally just happened to dissipate, but the gunners were quite convinced that it was their efforts that did the trick!

On July 15, 1871, the *Waverley* left Adelaide with strong westerlies on her quarter, and reached Sydney on 21st, for what is believed to be a record passage between the two ports. *Waverley* traded mostly between Adelaide, Melbourne and Sydney and later to Tasmanian ports, and was totally wrecked on the north Tasmanian coast in 1889.

But now the little clipper brig has gained perpetuity in that almost all Australians carry her likeness around with them in purses or wallets on the back of the Australian five dollar note, and if the eyesight is good enough her name, *Waverley*, can be read on the pennant flying proudly at her main truck.

THE LATTER DAYS OF SAIL

TOWARDS the end of the nineteenth century, the wool clippers were giving way to the steamship wool carriers, and it was obvious that the glorious era of sail was vanishing from the ports and oceans of the globe which they had served so well. The small wool carriers such as the ex-tea clippers were proving uneconomical on account of their lack of cargo capacity besides other economies forced on the sailing ships. Larger ships were chartered or built and the advent of the huge all steel ships with their steel sparring came to the fore to take their place in the Australian grain trade race for which they were suited. Sometimes an occasional wool coal or timber cargo would come their way, but mostly they sailed from Australian ports with grain. They were mighty ships, but sadly underman-ned. With their steel hulls down to their Plimsoll marks, their decks were continually awash in heavy weather and with a ridiculously small crew for the two watches of perhaps sixteen, this period was probably the hardest for the seamen in the long history of sail. The racing clippers of the '60s and '70s carried a crew of 30 or more for a vessel of 1,000 tons or less, but the grain ships of 2,000 to 3,000 tons or more meant a life of danger and hardship as never known before, and called for a special kind of courage and tenacity. The masters and officers were required to be superb seamen to compensate for their mostly inexperienced crews, especially when battling against the icy gales off Cape Horn.

In this region the terrific westerly squalls were known to seamen as Cape Horn snorters and the tremendous seas as Cape Horn greybeards. These terms are expressive of the wind that roars, groans and screams and of the great foam clad combers

L

The missionary ship *John Williams*, coming to anchor in Sydney Harbour.

which looked like rows of moving hills streaked with gigantic soapsuds and crested with gleaming snow. These seas have been measured by the sextant to a height of over 60 feet. At irregular intervals, a huge wave bigger than the rest advances in stately progress and on its flanks small waves foam in riotous confusion. Suddenly the head of the roller turns a translucent emerald green, grows steep, then breaks the length of its ridge into twenty feet of boiling surf.

When a ship's stern obstructs the path of such a giant wave, iron and steel are twisted like hairpins, stanchions of oak and teak are smashed, and often human bodies have been crushed to pulp.

To quote the great historian Basil Lubbock:—

"The sea breeds only one sort—The virile sort. The
sea is the great maker of men, men of courage and

grit, men of authority and resource, men of nerve, strength and muscle fitness. For fools she has no use nor for slackers nor the timid. These she either breaks or casts aside, and it has always been so. From the days of Noah, the sea has never bred a wastrel. Her men have bone and character, the firm lips of responsibility and the far seeing eyes of the distant horizon. Salt water produces nothing small, nothing petty, nothing insignificant".

Such was the character of seamen who being helpless were often swept the full length of decks by a heavy pooping sea over the stern, which in many instances meant a smashed wheel and broken limbs for the helmsman. In one instance a gigantic sea smashed the wheel down to the hub. The two helmsmen were later found, after the water had run off, under the mizzen fife rail, lying bleeding and insensible. The Captain and a seaman were washed overboard and lost.

Steering a ship under sail called for a special kind of sense acquired by some and never by others. The bigger the ship the more difficult she was to handle. Sometimes a bad helmsman allowed the ship to broach to, as when the wool clipper *Ben Voilich* lost nine men over the side. Two of them were washed off the lee fore yardarm as it dragged in the water. The *Inverclyde* went over until her topsail yardarms were in the water, and then it was "work for your lives" until cargo was jettisoned and trimmed. The *Torresdale* lay on her beam ends for two days with the seas breaking over her. The helmsmen of these ships were required to have nerves of steel. The later-built ships were wisely provided with a wheel house to protect the wheel and helmsman.

This account by Albert Sonnichsen, able seaman, from his "Deep Sea Vagabonds", gives an unforgettable pen picture:—
> "Before noon huge billowy masses of black clouds puffed up from the horizon to windward but the wind seemed lighter. The Captain went below while the mate was busy inspecting the ironwork about the decks from which men were chipping rust (another

Missionary barque *John Williams*, sails away from Sydney, with a favourable wind on the starboard quarter. She was to meet her fate, in the long line of missing ships.

chore for the seamen of the latter day steel ships). Shortly after, the watches were changed and the second mate came on deck while the chief went below for his dinner. The second mate was young and perhaps also, sleep lingered in his eyes. At any rate he saw not what he should have seen. Suddenly we, at our work were startled by a yell from the poop. It was an order from the second mate to do something, but the meaning of his words was drowned in a deep growling roar: the atmosphere chilled, a million hissing shrieking demons seemed tearing through the rigging, the vessel keeled over until her lee bulwarks were buried in a green and white sea that poured in on deck. Some of the men working on the weather side were sent flying across into a smother of foam. Overhead, sails were bursting or ripping with explosive reports; everywhere the atmosphere was thick with grey smothering spume. It truly seemed a battle of noises, the intermingling cannonading of banging sails, the incessant pealing of thunder and the wind, the awful screaming wind, louder than all. For one horrible moment, the decks retained that sickening slant, then very slowly, as though undecided, the vessel righted again. Most of the sails were fluttering in rags, of our mainsail only the leeches were left.

As the decks gradually assumed a horizontal position, all hands scattered about hauling down on clews and buntlines in bunches. We finally clewed up everything from the lower topsails. It took all hands some time to furl sail in that wind, but at last we crawled down on deck, we of the watch below expecting to be relieved. "Get your gear ready for reefing the fore upper topsail" shouted the mate. There were black looks and muttered curses. Reefing at the best is never a joke; in such a hurricane the humourous element of it is entirely missing, but the skipper thought only of a quick passsage. there were just twenty four men up on that yard, a dozen on each arm. As the sail was loosed the wind broke into it, and a huge white balloon swelled up, as hard as an iron shell. We might as well have tried to gather in the wind itself. The skipper on the poop saw how impossible was our task, so he ordered the man at the wheel to luff a trifle so that the strength of the wind might be taken out of the sail's belly. The cook was at the wheel and he was not an experienced seaman. It was too late when the skipper himself snatched the revolving spokes. The white mass gave a quiver, began to shiver, and then bang, bang, bang, it thundered and flapped, rolled up and down, smothered over the line of clinging men, pressing them to the yard, shaking the mast itself with mighty jerks. Just then one of the clews carried away, releasing the sail from the

Captain Airey of the iron barque *Rona*, in 1918. Built as the *Polly Woodside* in 1885, renamed *Rona* in 1904, this barque resumed her original name a few years ago when rescued from disintegration and she is now restored in Melbourne.

yard below. The heavy clew-iron and leech swished about like a whip, striking among the back stays and rigging. I heard a shriek, even above all this noise. A shower of drops flew past my eyes and spattered the struggling canvas before me, red. The man next to me was bleeding about the head, his sou'wester was gone and his hair was slimy red. Some irresistable influence caused me to look down. Before our forecastle door lay a figure in yellow oilskins, splotched with dark stains. Finally there came a momentary lull in the gale and, after an hour's struggle we did at last reef the sail, but the cost was paid in blood. From end to end the yard was covered in red handprints. When we came on deck the reefed sail was set and our watch went below. Toby one of the deck boys, had fallen from aloft and was badly injured. All the men on the lee yardarm were more or less cut and bruised. Gentile, the Italian, was gashed from eye to jaw.

All day and night the gale continued—on the second morning the storm was over.

That day there was sleep for no one; it was spent bending new canvas. By late in the afternoon the ship was once more on her course with all sails set".

To the master of a sailing ship fell the responsibility of controlling or curing the various diseases to which the men were subjected, such as scurvy, beri-beri, typhus and malaria plus other complaints.

During the eighteenth century, scurvy was the great killer. During Anson's voyage in 1741, his three ships with a total of 961 men finished up with only 335. It was known that once the men were ashore and fresh fruit and vegetables were available, they soon recovered.

The Dutch were the first to conceive the idea of vegetable gardens on board ship as a practical means of overcoming scurvy. In 1632, the *Grol* carried a garden of watercress, lettuce and radishes, but unfortunately this idea was discouraged by the high

Mrs. Airey, at the wheel of *Rona*.

Masters and Mates at the
navigation school in San Francisco.

seas which swept the decks. Nevertheless the Dutch were enterprising enough to provide stopping places on the voyage to the East Indies where fresh fruit and vegetables could be readily obtained.

Captain Cook applied himself to the problem of scurvy on his second voyage and with great success. His remedy was a thick syrup made in the form of a beer or wort, sauerkraut, and the juice of lemons and oranges boiled down to the consistency of syrup. However, some of the crew developed scurvy much to Cook's alarm, but on enquiry he found that the failing ones were dodging the issue, so Cook applied some strict naval discipline and the would-be dodgers soon recovered.

Another great navigator learned much from Cook and put his teachings into practice. Captain Vancouver, commander of the *Discovery* and after whom the city of Vancouver and Vancouver Island British Columbia are named, had several years experience with Captain Cook. From him Vancouver learned that a good commander takes care of his men and from him he learned how.

Eventually during the nineteenth century the Board of Trade substituted the lime for the lemon. Every man on board a British ship was required to drink a pannikin of lime juice at 8 bells midday and of course every British ship was known as a limejuicer. Unfortunately, medical men have since proved that the lime has none of the anti-scorbutic properties.

Sailing vessels were regarded by the sailors as hungry ships. They lived on their 'bare whack' (nautical term for allowance by law). The main article of diet was Liverpool pantiles and was the subject of much debate amongst the Foc's'cle crowd as to their composition. An old shellback was of the opinion that they were composed of paper pulp. Burgoo, salt pork, and salt beef were staples, but the allowance for sustenance added up to an unsatisfying short ration.

The sailor endured and survived the perils of life at sea, only to face up to more perils on arrival in port. In most of the large ports the master had to pay so much a head to the crimps in order to complete their crews. These parasites, the crimps and their

Four masted barque *Bermuda*, showing her magnificent run of deck.
(Photograph, San Francisco Maritime Museum).

runners, induced the happy-go-lucky shellbacks to desert ship for the sake of a night of revelry on shore. As soon as the anchors were down the boarding house runners were alongside and, dodging the officers, hid themselves in the foc's'cle until the crew came off duty. As soon as it was dark those who were ready to desert were taken ashore in boats. Once ashore in the crimps' clutches they were plied with bad liquor or maybe drugged or sandbagged and in a day or two shipped away in a state of insensibility.

Not all sailors deserted their ships and many sailed on the same ship with the same captain for years. Such was the life of the sailor. They toiled and endured but there were compensations. They were carefree and during the tropic nights in flying fish weather they could lie on the hatch watching the stars through the rigging and swap yarns.

They developed a companionship which was among men of different nationalities, and, for them, frontiers did not exist. They learned to respect each others' viewpoints on the fore hatch or foc's'cle in the dog watches during fine weather sailing. With a wind in the quarter and all sails drawing, perhaps an accordian or mouth organ was brought to light, followed by a 'sing-song'.

Tough, virile and courageous, they were a special breed of men. They had to be, in order to survive. They had their own type of humour, as illustrated by the old seaman who was asked, "Did you have a wife in every port, Captain?" "Certainly not", he roared, "I haven't been in every port!"

EPILOGUE

THE ships mentioned in this book are but a small cross-section of the wide panorama of sailing ships which plied their trade between the hemispheres thus keeping a bond between the old and new world. The book is dedicated to the men who designed, built and sailed the clipper ships that reached the pinnacle of grace and beauty.

Opening of the Suez Canal, in 1869. This hastened the end of the sailing tea clippers. Steamers were able to complete the voyage in half the time.

GLOSSARY OF NAUTICAL TERMS

Aback:—When the wind presses the sails against the masts and forces the vessel astern.

Abaft:—Towards the stern of a vessel.

About:—On the other tack.

A-cock-bill:—When the yards are topped up at an angle with the deck.

Aft:—Near the stern.

A-lee:—When the helm is put in the opposite direction from that in which the wind blows.

Aloft:—Above the deck.

Aloof:—At a distance.

Amidships:—In the centre of a vessel.

Anchor watch:—A small watch of one or two men, kept while in port.

Astern:—In the direction of the stern.

A-trip:—When an anchor is raised clear of the ground.

Avast:—Order to stop.

A-Weather:—When the helm is put in the direction from which the wind blows.

A-weigh:—The same as a-trip.

Ballast:—Heavy material as lead, iron or stone placed in the holds to keep a vessel from upsetting.

Belay:—To make a rope fast by turns around a pin, without seizing it.

Belaying pin:—Wood or metal handled pins, inserted in the pin rail. Used for belaying running rigging.

Beating:—Going towards the direction of the wind by alternate tacks.

Before the wind:—Sailing with the wind blowing after the ship.

Bend:—To make fast; to bend a sail is to make it fast to the yard (unbend: to cast off).

Bill:—The points of the fluke of an anchor.

Bill-boards:—To protect the ships plank's from the bill of the anchor.

Billet Head:—The work at the prow of a vessel; simple carved work bending over and out (see fiddle head).

Binnacle:—A box or stand near the helm containing the mariner's compass.

Bitts:—Perpendicular pieces of timber going through the deck; placed to fasten anything to.

Bitter end:—The inboard end of the cable secured in the chain locker (when a ship is riding out a gale at anchor, she may pay out more cable to ease the strain, even to the bitter end).

Boatswain:—Pronounced Bo's'n. Petty officer and head man of the crew.

Bobstay:—Used to confine the bowsprit down to the stem. Chain or iron. (The most important stay in a ship. If that gives way, generally means partial or total dismastings).

Boltrope:—A rope sewn around the edges of a sail to strengthen it.

Bowline:—(Pronounced bolin) A rope leading forward from the leech of a square sail to keep the leech well out in order to catch the wind when sailing close-hauled.

Braces:—Ropes leading from the yardarms to the vessel's side or adjacent masts by means of which the yards are hauled to any required position.

Broach to:—To be turned violently at right angles to a following sea.

Bulwark:—The wood work (or iron) around a vessel above her deck fastened to timber heads or stanchions.

Bunt:—The middle of a sail.

Buntlines:—Ropes used for hauling up the body of a sail.

Caboose:—Cook house or galley.

Careen:—To heave a vessel down on her sides by purchases on the masts. (Usually for the purpose of cleaning or repairing the bottom).

Cat:—The tackle used to hoist an anchor to the cathead.

Cat-head:—Large timbers projecting from the ship's sides to which the anchor is raised and secured. Decorated with a cat's face on the end.

Chains:—Cables; also strong links or plates of iron fastened to the ship's side extending to the channels.

Chain plates:—Plates of iron bolted to the sides of a ship to which the chains and dead eyes of the lower rigging are connected.

Channels:—Broad pieces of plank bolted edgewise to the outside of a vessel. Used for spreading the lower rigging.

Condenser:—Apparatus for producing fresh water from salt water.

Clew:—The lower corner of square sails, and the after corner of a fore and aft.

Clew garnet:—A rope that hauls up the clew of a foresail or main course in a square rigged vessel.

Clew lines:—The rope that hauls up the clews of the upper sails to their respective yards.

Crown:—Of an anchor where the arms are joined to the shank.

Close-hauled:—Applied to a vessel which is sailing with her yards braced up so as to get as much to windward as possible (full and by; on the wind).

Dead eyes:—Circular wooden blocks with three holes through which are reeved the lanyards used for setting up the shrouds and backstays. Round the outer circumference is a groove for an iron strap.

Dead reckoning:—A reckoning kept by observing a vessel's course and distances by the log to ascertain her position.

Deadweight:—Deadweight tonnage, ship's carrying capacity in tons.

Dog watch:—Half watches of two hours each, from 4 p.m. to 6 p.m. and from 6 p.m. to 8 p.m. (see watch).

Dog vane:—A small vane made from feathers or bunting to show the direction of the wind.

Dolphin Striker:—An iron or wood spar secured to outer end of bowsprit. (see martingale).

Downhaul:—A rope used to haul down jibs, staysails and stunsails.

Earing:—A term given to the outer corners of the head of a square sail, also the rope or line by means of which the corner is lashed to the yard (sometimes known as a bullwhanger).

Fag:—A rope is fagged when the end is untwisted.

Fall:—That part of a tackle to which force is applied on hoisting.

Falling off:—The vessel's head turning more to leeward.

Fathom:—Six feet.

Fiddle head:—Carved work at the bow, extremity bending in like the head of a violin.

Fife rail:—The rail going around the mast; fitted with belaying pins.

Figurehead:—A carved head or full length figure over the cutwater.

Fish:—To raise the flukes of an anchor upon the rail. Also to strengthen a spar when split or sprung.

Fish tackle:—The tackle used for fishing an anchor.

Flare:—When the vessel's side or bows curve outwards in the upward direction.

Flemish horse:—An additional foot rope at the extreme end of a yard..

Flukes:—The broad triangular plates at the extremity of the arms of an anchor.

Footrope:—The rope stretching along and underneath a yard upon which men stand when reefing or furling.

Fore:—The forward part of a ship (forrard).

Fore and aft:—Lengthwise with the vessel.

Forecastle:—Pronounced Fo'c'sle. The forward part of the vessel where the sailors live.

Fother:—To draw a sail filled with oakum under a ship's bottom in order to stop a leak.

Free:—A vessel is going free when she has a fair wind and her yards braced in.

Freeboard:—The distance from the main deck to the water's edge.

Full and by:—Sailing close hauled on a wind; the order given to the man at the helm to keep the sails full and not allow the leech of the sail to shake.

Furl:—To roll a sail up snugly on a yard or boom and secure it.

Galley:—Where the cooking is done (caboose).

Gallows-bitts:—A strong frame raised amidships to support spare spars.

Gaskets:—Rope or pieces of plaited stuff, used to secure a sail to the yards or boom when it is furled.

Goose winged:—The situation of a course when the buntlines and the lee clews are hauled up and the weather clew down.

Goring cloths:—Pieces cut in obliquely and put in to add to the breadth of a sail.

Gripe:—A piece of timber fitted on the lower part of the stem.

Ground tackle:—General term for anchors, cables etc.

Gripes:—For lashing down boats.

Gudgeons:—Metal braces with eyes bolted on the stern post for the pintles of the rudder to work in.

Guntackle purchase:—A purchase made from two single blocks.

Gunwale:—(Pronounced gun-nel) The upper rail of a boat.

Guy:—A rope attaching to anything to steady it.

Gybe:—(Or gibe) To shift over the boom of a fore and aft sail.

Halyards:—(Halliards) Rope or tackles used for hoisting and lowering yards.

Handspike:—A long wooden bar used for heaving at the windlass.

Hanks:—Rings around a stay seized to the luff of a fore and aft sail.

Hard down:—The order to put the tiller hard over to leeward; hard up, to put it hard over to windward.

Harness casks:—Two casks secured and locked, containing salt beef in one, salt pork in the other.

Hatch or hatchway:—An opening in the deck to afford a passage up and down. Coverings are called hatches.

Hawse hole:—The hole in the bows through which the cable runs.

Haze:—A term of punishment by keeping a man on disagreeable or difficult duty.

Heart:—A block of wood in the shape of a heart for stays to reeve through.

Heave short:—To heave in the cable until the vessel is nearly over her anchor.

Helm:—The machinery by which a vessel is steered including the rudder, tiller and wheel etc.

Hogged:—The state of a vessel when by any strain she droops at each end, causing an upward arching at the centre of the keel.

Holystone:—A large abrasive stone used for cleaning decks.

Jackstays:—Ropes stretched taut along a yard to bend the head of a sail to, also long strips of wood or iron used for the same purpose.

Jettison:—The act of throwing cargo overboard.

Jolly boat:—A small boat usually hoisted at the stern.

Keel haul:—To haul a man under a vessel's bottom by ropes at the yardarms on each side.

Knot:—A division on the log-line answering to a mile of distance. Also a speed measure of one nautical mile per hour.

Landfall:—A good landfall is when a vessel sights the land as intended.

Lanyards:—Rope rove through dead-eyes for setting up rigging.

Lay:—To come or to go; as lay aloft; lay forward; lay aft. Lay is also the direction in which the strands of a rope are twisted—left to right or right to left.

Leech:—The vertical edges of a sail.

Leech lines:—Ropes leading from the leeches of a square sail through blocks above the yards and down to the deck, and used to control and gather in the sail for furling.

Lee:—The side opposite to that from which the wind blows as, if a vessel has the wind on her starboard side that will be the weather, and the port will be the lee side. A lee shore is on the side of the ship opposite that from which the wind is blowing.

Leeward:—(Pronounced Lu-ard) The lee side.

Lift:—A rope or tackle going from the yardarms to the mast head, to support and move the yard.

Log:—Or Log Book. A Journal kept by the chief officer in which the situation of the vessel, wind weather course, distances and everything of importance that occurs is noted down.

Log Line:—The principle of the log line is that a knot bears the same proportion to a sea mile that a 14 second glass does to one hour of time. Log lines, in fast sailing ships, are usually 75 fathoms in length; this allows the log to have 15 fathoms of stray line and records the vessel's speed up to 15 knots per hour when using the 14 second glass.

Long boat:—The largest boat in a merchant vessel. When at sea it is carried between the fore and main masts.

Luff:—To put the helm so as to bring the ship up nearer the wind.

Marl:—To wind or twist a small line or rope around another.

Marline:—(Pronounced Mar-lin) Small 2-stranded stuff used for marling.

Martingale:—A short perpendicular spar under the bowsprit used to give greater spread to the stays below the bowsprit. Gives additional strength to bowsprit and jibboom and counteracts the upward pull of the headstays. (Same as dolphin striker).

Miss stays:—To fail going about from one tack to another.

Normans:—Stout pieces of iron placed in the holes of a windlass to prevent the chain fouling as it runs out.

Oakum:—Material made by picking rope-yarn to pieces; old rope untwisted and loosened like hemp; used for caulking.

Palm:—A piece of leather fitted over the hand with an iron for the head of a needle to press against in sewing canvas. Also the fluke of an anchor.

Parcel:—To wind tarred canvas around a rope is called parcelling.

Parrel:—A band to hold a hoisting yard to the mast.

Pawl:—A short bar of iron which prevents the capstan or windlass from turning back.

Pinrail:—A rail fixed inside the bulwarks with holes for belaying pins .

Pintle:—A metal bolt used for swinging a rudder.

Pole:—Applied to the highest mast of a ship, usually painted white.

Poop:—A deck raised over the after part of the ship. A vessel is 'pooped' when the sea breaks over her stern.

Port:—The left side of a ship when looking forward. To 'port the helm' is to put it to the port side of the ship.

Quarter:—That part of the ship's side between the centre of the stern and the mizzen lowermast shrouds. Wind on the port or starboard quarter is the best angle for fast sailing.

Quarter deck:—That part of the upper deck abaft the mainmast.

Racking:—To seize two ropes together with cross turns.

Ratlines:—(Pronounced ratlins) Lines running across the shrouds horizontally like the rungs of a ladder for stepping aloft.

Reef:—To reduce a sail by tying part of it up on its yard.

Reef band:—A band of stout canvas sewed on the sail across to provide extra strength at the reef points.

Reef Points:—The lines used when reefing. They pass through eyelets on the band, are of equal length and tie the reefed portion of sail to the yard.

Reef tackle:—A tackle used to haul up the middle of each leech towards the yard so that the sail may be reefed.

Ride:—To lie at anchor.

Rigging:—The general term for all the ropes of a ship.

Ring tail:—A small sail set abaft the spanker.

Roach:—A curve in the foot of square sail.

Run:—The narrowing of the hull of a ship aft.

Running rigging:—The ropes that move through blocks and are pulled and hauled, such as braces, halyards, clewlines, buntlines, etc.

Sagged:—The middle part of the keel lower than the ends; opposite of hogged.

Scud:—To drive before a gale, with no sail, or only enough to keep the vessel ahead of the sea.

Scuppers:—Holes bored through the water ways for the water to run from the decks.

Seams:—The spaces between planks on a vessel's deck or side.

Serve:—To wind spun yarn round a rope to prevent chafing. It is wound and hove round taut by a serving mallet.

Shackles:—Links in a chain cable fitted with a moveable bolt in order to separate the chains.

Shank:—The main piece of an anchor.

Sharp up:—When yards are braced as near fore and aft as possible.

Sheathing:—A protective covering or casing on a ship's bottom to prevent fouling, consisting of copper or muntz metal plates 4 ft.$\times$14 ins. fastened on with copper nails.

Sheave:—The wheel in a block upon which the rope works.

Sheer pole:—A piece of iron across the rigging above the upper dead eye and seized to each shroud.

Sheet:—A rope or chain used in setting a sail to keep the clew down to its place.

Shrouds:—The standing rigging between the lower masthead and the ship's sides. Also from topmast head and the rim of the top, also topgallant masthead and the topmast crosstrees.

Spars:—The general term for all masts, yards, booms, gaffs, etc.

Spencer:—A fore and aft sail set with a gaff and no boom abaft the fore and mainmasts.

Stanchions:—Upright posts of wood or iron placed to support bulwarks or railings.

Standing rigging:—The part of a vessel's rigging which is made fast and not hauled upon (see running).

Starboard:—The right side of a vessel looking forward.

Stay:—To tack a vessel or to put her about so that the wind from being on one side is brought upon the other, round the vessel's head.

Stays:—Large ropes (wire or hemp) used to support masts. Fore stays, which lead forward, and backstays (from mastheads to the side of the ship).

Steeves:—A bowsprit and jibboom steeves, up or down, from the horizon.

Stern-board:—Or stern way, when a ship is moving stern first.

Stiff:—The quality of a vessel which enables it to carry a great deal of sail without lying too much on her side. The opposite to crank.

Stirrups:—Short ropes extending from jackstays to abaft the yard at regular intervals to support the foot ropes.

Stock:—A beam of wood or a bar of iron secured to the upper end of the shank at right angles. An iron stock is usually fitted with a key and can be unshipped.

Stocks:—The frame upon which a vessel is built.

Strap:—A piece of rope spliced around a block.

Studding sails:—Light sails set outside the square sails on yards and booms. They are only carried with a fair wind and moderate weather.

Swifter:—The forward shroud to a lower mast.

Tack:—To put a ship about (see stay). Also the rope or tackle by which the weather clew of a course is brought forward and down to the deck.

Tackle:—(Pronounced taycle) A purchase formed by a rope rove through two blocks.

Taffrail:—The rail housed on stanchions around the poop.

Tar (Stockholm):—Liquid gum taken from pine and fir trees and used for caulking, parcelling, serving and for water-proofing ropes.

Tender:—Opposite to stiff.

Tonnage:—Gross tonnage is a measure of the volume of a ship including all cargo carrying space and space for passenger and crew accommodation (excluding certain exempted spaces); one "ton" is 100 cubic feet.

Net tonnage is also a measure of volume and is arrived at by deducting crew space and certain other designated spaces from the gross tonnage.

Top:—A platform over the head of the lower mast. It rests on the trestle trees and spreads the rigging.

Touch:—A vessel is said to touch when the wind strikes the leech so that it shakes a little. 'Luff and touch her' is the order to bring a vessel up, to see how near the wind she will go.

Trick:—The time allotted to a man to stand at the wheel, usually two hours.

Trim:—The condition of a vessel when her cargo and ballast are placed well for sailing. To trim is to place cargo or ballast nearer the head or stern.

Truck:—A circular piece of wood placed at the head of each pole mast. It has small holes or sheaves for signal halliards.

Waist:—The part of the deck between the quarter deck and the forecastle.

Waisters:—'Green' hands or broken-down seamen stationed to work in the waist of a vessel.

Wake:—The track or path the ship leaves behind her in the water.

Warp:—To haul a ship by a rope attached to a fixed object.

Watch:—A division of time on board ship. There are seven watches in a 24 hour day; five are four hours each and two, called the dog watches are from 4 p.m. to 6 p.m. and from 6 p.m. to 8 p.m. In the merchant service all hands are divided into two watches, port and starboard, and a mate commands each.

Wear:—A vessel when close hauled wears ship by turning away from the wind and adjusting yards and sails to sail up the wind again with the wind on the other side.

Weather:—A weatherly ship is one that works well to windward and makes little leeway; also the side of a ship on which the wind is blowing.

Weigh:—To lift up the anchor from the sea-bed.

Whip:—A purchase formed by a rope rove through a single block.

Windlass:—A machine for weighing the anchor.

Worm:—To fill up between the lay of the rope with small rope yarns wound spirally.

Yard:—A spar slung at its centre from and forward of a mast. It is used to support and extend square sails.

Yaw:—The motion of a vessel when she goes from side to side off course owing to bad steering, or from effects of a seaway.

TIMES OF THE WATCHES

The day of twenty-four hours is divided into seven watches:

Noon to 4 p.m.	afternoon watch
4 p.m. to 6 p.m.	first dog watch
6 p.m. to 8 p.m.	second dog watch
8 p.m. to midnight	first watch
midnight to 4 a.m.	middle watch
4 a.m. to 8 a.m.	morning watch
8 a.m. to noon	forenoon watch

The time is denoted on board ship by striking a bell every half hour, the rule being: one stroke of the bell at half past four; half past eight; half past twelve. One more stroke is added for each half hour until eight strokes of the bell, or eight bells, are reached at four, eight and twelve (a.m. and p.m.).

The dog watches are different:
(First dog watch)

4.30 p.m.	one stroke
5 p.m.	two strokes
5.30 p.m.	three strokes
6 p.m.	four strokes

(Second dog watch)

6.30 p.m.	one stroke
7 p.m.	two strokes
7.30 p.m.	three strokes
8 p.m.	eight strokes

Eight bells are four double strokes. This system now obsolete.

RAISING ANCHOR

IN raising anchor, with the other anchor still out, the cable of the latter was slackened off from around the barrel and triced up to the strongback above.

In heaving in, it was necessary as the chain wound itself along the barrel to stopper it, and fleet the chain back again. Another very necessary procedure was to station a hand with a luff tackle abaft the windlass to keep the chain taut to prevent it slipping back and thus losing a hard won pawl or turn on the purchase rim.

As soon as the anchor broke surface the three fold cat fall was attached to the anchor ring and hoisted close to the cat head.

The fish tackle was then hooked to a fluke and the anchor hoisted to the bill board and onto the Foc's'cle deck.

At sea the cable was unshackled from the anchor and stowed back into the chain lockers.

The fish tackle, a three fold purchase, was secured to the topmast head for the purpose of hoisting the anchor over the side where it was suspended by the cat stopper under the cat head

Sketch by Captain Carter of Sydney showing typical windlass; known facetiously as "Armstrong's patent" because it needed strong arms to operate.

ready for letting go. The cat stopper consisted of a chain with the standing end fastened to the cat head passing through the ring of the anchor and then up to the anchor releasing gear set up on the other side of the cat head. The anchor was now cock-billed and ready for the order "let go".

The anchor release gear was a device usually operated by the ship's carpenter, which consisted of a pin which was tripped by a lever or maul allowing the cat stopper chain to run free.

When the order was given "Let go", the anchor struck ground and the ship moved slowly forward until the slack of the chain was taken up and it tightened around the barrel.

This was accompanied by a terrific racket and clatter with sparks flying as the cable slipped around the iron whelps and snaked off the main deck on to the barrel. The resultant friction finally caused the ship to lose way and the cable was stoppered abaft the hawse, taking the strain of riding at anchor, off the windlass.

Photograph of the break of the fo'c'stle on a ship not fitted with a windlass

OLD FASHIONED BARREL WINDLASS

"**M**AIN strength", "Armstrong's patent", a "rope yarn over a rail"; such were the disparaging names by the old shellbacks in referring to the piece of machinery known as the barrel windlass. Up and down, with the levers, up and down, tip toe when the lever was up and watch your toes when the lever was down. With 45 fathom of cable out, it was four hours of back breaking work for the poor sailor and his shipmates, a kind of treadmilling experience they would never forget. Nevertheless, the windlass fulfilled its function efficiently enough and it was certainly endurable. On many old hulks with the decks swept clean of other machinery, deck houses and bulwarks, etc., it still stood out as a challenge to the ravages of time. The constructional details were of necessity extremely strong and sturdy, designed to withstand the strain of the heavy duty required. Of no fixed standard dimensions, it was built to suit the construction of the ship and varied somewhat in length according to width of deck, and formed an integral part of the ship's bows. The centre or pawl bitt of hardwood carried down to the beams of the 'tween decks and even to the keelson in smaller vessels. The barrel, also of hardwood, was faced with iron strips or whelps to withstand the friction of the cables running out. The bearings of the barrel spindle were mounted on the carrick bitts of green heart, the strongest timber available. They, in turn, were supported by tremendous knees on the for'ard side to counteract the weight of both cable and anchor. The anchor cable passed on through the hawse hole, over the top of the barrel with three turns and then aft to the chain lockers through the spurling pipes. The chain locker consisted of an iron tank situated on the keelson at the foot of the foremast or mainmast (as did *Thermopylae*'s). It was divided by a fore and aft partition into two, one for the port cable and the other for the starboard.

COMING TO AN ANCHOR

A day or so before reaching soundings, the cables were hove up from the chain lockers and ranged on deck, and according to the depth of anchorage, anything to 100 fathoms for either anchor. The cables were hauled forward for the three turns over the barrel windlass out through the hawse pipe and shackled to the anchors. Enough free chain was ranged on deck for'ard of the windlass at the first turn, and again at the middle turn, to ensure that the anchors reached ground with the cable running freely between the barrel and the hawse pipe. This was most essential because, if the cable tightened around the barrel before the anchor reached bottom, the resultant strain would either break the barrel or the cable or cause other serious damage. The rest of the cable was ranged up and down the main deck abaft the windlass ready for running. The normans were also shipped ready. These consisted of two iron bars fitted into holes on the windlass barrel between the first turn and the middle, and between the middle turn and the third. This was to prevent the cables from riding over each other and fouling. A ship was usually brought to her anchorage under upper topsails or main upper topsail only, (according to wind) and with spanker and headsail.

The ship was required to have a little headway over the ground to ensure that the cable ran out clear without fouling the anchor.

INDEX

Page   Page